# PROPERTY DISPUTES IN PRACTICE

# PROPERTY DISPUTES
# IN PRACTICE

## Inns of Court School of Law

BLACKSTONE
PRESS LIMITED

First published in Great Britain 1998 by Blackstone Press Limited,
Aldine Place, London W12 8AA. Telephone (020) 8740 2277
www.blackstonepress.com


© Inns of Court School of Law, 1998


First edition 1998
Second edition 1999
Third edition 2000


ISBN: 1 84174 006 3


British Library Cataloguing in Publication Data
A CIP catalogue record for this book is available from the British Library.


Typeset by Style Photosetting Ltd, Mayfield, East Sussex
Printed by Ashford Colour Press, Gosport, Hampshire

# FOREWORD

These manuals are designed primarily to support training on the Bar Vocational Course, though they are also intended to provide a useful resource for legal practitioners and for anyone undertaking training in legal skills.

The Bar Vocational Course was designed by staff at the Inns of Court School of Law, where it was introduced in 1989. This course is intended to equip students with the practical skills and the procedural and evidential knowledge that they will need to start their legal professional careers. These manuals are written by staff at the Inns of Court School of Law who have helped to develop the course, and by a range of legal practitioners and others involved in legal skills training. The authors of the manuals are very well aware of the practical and professional approach that is central to the Bar Vocational Course.

The range and coverage of the manuals have grown steadily. All the practice manuals are updated every two years, and regular reviews and revisions of the manuals are carried out to ensure that developments in legal skills training and the experience of our staff are fully reflected in them.

This updating and revision is a constant process, and we very much value the comments of practitioners, staff and students. Legal vocational training is advancing rapidly, and it is important that all those concerned work together to achieve and maintain high standards. Please address any comments to the Bar Vocational Course Director at the Inns of Court School of Law.

With the validation of other providers for the Bar Vocational Course it is very much our intention that these manuals will be of equal value to all students wherever they take the course, and we would value comments from tutors and students at other validated institutions.

The enthusiasm of the staff at Blackstone Press Ltd and their efficiency in arranging the production and publication of these manuals is much appreciated.

*The Hon. Mr Justice Elias*
*Chairman of the Board of Governors*
*Inns of Court School of Law*
*December 1999*

# CONTENTS

# CONTENTS

# TABLE OF CASES

# TABLE OF CASES

# TABLE OF STATUTES

# INTRODUCTION

This manual covers the main types of property actions likely to be encountered in general Chancery practice. Because of the breadth of the subject, it can only give an overview highlighting areas of particular importance or interest.

A knowledge of land law can be important in a surprisingly large number of areas of practice. Disputes over whether a transfer of land has been properly effected, or whether some third party has acquired rights over an owner's land, can often crop up in what appeared to be an ordinary commercial contracts dispute and many divorce cases require some understanding of how interests in land can be transferred and protected. Junior Chancery practitioners can expect to deal with some minor or major issue involving interests in land in many of their cases. Even if practitioners are called upon to deal with a straightforward-seeming mortgage possession, it is necessary for them to have a sound grasp of how title to property and equitable rights are acquired, so that they can check on the respective rights of parties, and possible parties.

Land law is both case and statute based and it will often be necessary to refer to the main statutes (collected in *Current Law Statutes Annotated* or in *Halsbury's Statutes of England and Wales*). Once you have established what is likely to be the main problem in the case with which you are dealing, it is often necessary to read the full text of one or two cases, but to identify the relevant cases it is usually necessary to resort to textbooks first. If your study of land law so far has been very academically orientated (or at the other extreme confined to examination crib texts), Mackenzie and Phillips, *A Practical Approach to Land Law*, is a useful introduction to the practical basics. Megarry and Wade, *The Law of Real Property*, is much used by practitioners for more detailed coverage. To understand how the conveyancing process should work in most circumstances it is helpful to refer to one of the works aimed at aspiring solicitors, e.g. *LPC Guide: Conveyancing*, Blackstone Press. Once an overview has been obtained, reference should be made to the specialist text in that area. Some of the most important are: *Emmet on Title*; *Ruoff and Roper on Registered Conveyancing*; *Woodfall on Landlord and Tenant*; and *Snell's Equity*.

Trusts is another area of law which has a habit of turning up when you least expect it. Any of the standard student texts, such as Hanbury and Martin, are a good starting point but it is then usually necessary to refer to a more comprehensive text such as *Snell on Equity*, *Tudor on Charities*, *Underhill on Wills* or *Williams on Wills*.

# ONE

# TITLE TO AND TRANSFERS OF LAND

## 1.1 General

Junior Chancery barristers will sometimes be called upon to draft contracts or transfers of land, particularly where a transfer of interests in land is part of a settlement of a case, or trustees in bankruptcy are involved or other special circumstances exist. More often the barrister's advice is sought when something has gone wrong and a conveyance has not proceeded as planned, or a difference of opinion arises at a later date over the terms of the transfer. Additionally, if you are dealing with any dispute about the use of land, for example in the context of planning regulations, trustees' powers and duties, co-ownership claims or neighbour disputes, it is first necessary to try to discover who holds the legal estate of which land, and from whom they acquired their title.

### 1.1.1 RESEARCHING AND DEFINING THE PROBLEM

In advising on a dispute about ownership, to try to establish who is the legal owner, the first place to look is obviously the Land Registry certificate if the land is registered or the latest conveyance which can be found if it is not.

If it is alleged that the land certificate or the latest conveyance does not record the true legal owner then it is necessary to identify what sort of difficulty appears to have arisen.

#### 1.1.1.1 Formalities

Is the problem essentially one of formalities, i.e., there is no real dispute that the person named is not the current legal owner but there is a question about whether the alleged new owner can give good title? The sorts of situations where this might arise are where the registered owner has died or the registered owners are trustees (probably charitable trustees) and one or more have died or retired possibly with other people alleged to have taken their places.

If a non-trustee legal owner has died and the alleged new owner has a certificate of probate, you need to go no further. Otherwise you need to look at any will left and if there is no will what happens to the estate under the rules of intestate succession. Then for the form of the documents required, see *Emmet on Title*. If the registered owners are trustees and two of the people named are claiming to be able to give good title, a purchaser has no difficulty, but otherwise it is necessary to look at the trust deed to see how new trustees can be appointed and any other documents purporting to appoint new trustees or purporting to be a retirement by a former trustee. Then for the form of documents required and the consequences of non-compliance, see *Emmet on Title*.

Since the Land Registration Act 1997, s. 1, came into force it is necessary to consider, in cases of transfer by way of gift where the land is not already registered, whether first registration should have taken place and the consequences of non-compliance.

### 1.1.1.2    Change of circumstance

Is the allegation that the documents do not reflect the true position due to recent events? First establish what kind of change is alleged to have taken place — gift, bankruptcy, sale. Then check what formalities are required and whether they appear to have been complied with. See **1.2** for a basic outline and further *Emmet on Title* and *Ruoff and Roper on Registered Land*. If a dispute has arisen between a valid contract for sale having been signed and a conveyance taking place, see **1.6** on whether there is any valid argument to counter the basic rule that the non-defaulting party is entitled to insist that the conveyance takes place and that that person is the new legal owner.

### 1.1.1.3    Adverse possession

Is the allegation that events over a longer period have altered the position as reflected in the Land Registry certificate or latest conveyance? The answer will then turn on the application of the law on adverse possession. First it is necessary to establish from oral and any documentary and photographic evidence:

(a)    what acts are relied upon;

(b)    what is the nature of the land and possible uses of it;

(c)    whether the 'legal owner' had objected or given permission for the alleged activities to have taken place;

(d)    if the alleged acts of adverse possession cover a continuous period of over 12 years.

Then consider whether as a matter of law the alleged acts are capable of being acts of adverse possession: see **1.5.5** and *Megarry and Wade on Real Property*.

## 1.2    Transfer of Legal Estate in Land

A transfer of a legal estate in land takes place in two stages: first, the contract; second, the conveyance or grant.

### 1.2.1    THE CONTRACT

The rules relating to contracts for the sale of land were amended by the Law of Property (Miscellaneous Provisions) Act 1989. The date of the contract determines which rules apply.

### 1.2.1.1    Contracts made before 28 September 1989

The contract must be *evidenced* in writing, in order to be enforceable: Law of Property Act (LPA) 1925, s. 40(1). Note that the contract remains valid though unenforceable. For the position with respect to deposits paid under such contracts, see dictum of Nicholls V-C in *Boddington* v *Lawton* [1994] ICR 478. Contracts which do not comply with s. 40(1) will be enforceable if there are sufficient acts of part performance: s. 40(2). What must be shown is that the acts in question are such as must be referred to some contract, and may be referred to the alleged one; that they prove the existence of some contract and are consistent with the contract alleged: *Steadman* v *Steadman* [1976] AC 536.

### 1.2.1.2    Contracts made on or after 28 September 1989

The contract must be *made* in writing and contain all the terms of the agreement and must be signed by all the parties (counterparts separately signed may be used): Law of Property (Miscellaneous Provisions) Act 1989, s. 2. Typing of a name is not sufficient. The appropriate document has to be signed by an individual in his or her own handwriting: *Firstpost Homes Ltd* v *Johnson* [1995] 4 All ER 355, CA. The equitable doctrine of part performance does not apply. Short leases under the LPA 1925 are not covered by s. 2 of the 1989 Act; these may be made in the same way as any other contract.

A party cannot complain after completion that the contract did not comply with s. 2: the section applies only to executory, still uncompleted contracts: *Tootal Clothing Ltd* v *Guinea Properties Management Ltd* (1992) 64 P & CR 452, CA. Consequently, s. 2 does not apply to executed contracts: *Target Holdings Ltd* v *Priestley* (1999) 96(14) LSG 33. General principles of collateral contracts may be prayed in aid to circumvent the requirement that all the terms must be set out in the contract or in documents referred to in the contract: see, for example, *Record* v *Bell* [1991] 1 WLR 853. A problem area is that of subsequent oral variations of the contract. Section 2 has been held not to apply to variations to a pre-existing contract: *McCausland* v *Duncan Lawrie Ltd* [1997] 1 WLR 38. Note also the difficulties which may be caused as regards *contracts related to land sales*: a lock-out agreement (whereby a vendor promises a potential purchaser that he will not consider other offers for a certain period) is not a contract for the sale of land and is not covered by the requirements of s. 2: *Pitt* v *PHH Asset Management* [1994] 1 WLR 327, CA. In contrast, in *Wright* v *Robert Leonard (Developments)* [1994] NPC 49, CA, it was held that a contract for the sale of house furnishings was so interlinked with the sale of the land as to form a single transaction. Section 2, therefore, did apply. (However, on the facts rectification was available.)

## 1.2.2 GRANT

The conveyance, grant or transfer of land or of any interest in land must be by deed and is void if not: Law of Property Act 1925, s. 52. Leases for terms not exceeding three years are an exception and may be created orally or in writing: LPA 1925, s. 4(2). It is also possible to acquire freehold title by use – title by adverse possession and an easement by prescription (see **1.5.5**). The requirement that deeds must be sealed was abolished with effect from 31 July 1990: Law of Property (Miscellaneous Provisions) Act 1989, s. 1. It is sufficient if a deed is signed, in the presence of a witness, and delivered.

# 1.3 Conveyancing

In any dispute involving conveyancing, the first question to be addressed is whether the land is registered or unregistered. There are significant differences between the two systems of conveyancing, both on a conceptual and a practical level. These differences may well affect the way in which an action should be framed. It is, for example, a general rule that a forged document is a nullity. Accordingly, in unregistered land, a forged document does not pass title; an appropriate remedy would be a declaration that such was the case. In registered land, however, a forged transfer would procure the registration of the 'purchaser'. Registration vests good title in the person registered: Land Registration Act (LRA) 1925, s. 20(1). Accordingly the appropriate remedy is for rectification, in order to divest the 'purchaser' of good title, improperly obtained.

## 1.3.1 REGISTERED LAND

Since 1990, it has been compulsory throughout England and Wales, to register fees simple and leases of more than 21 years. The Land Registration Act 1997 provides that compulsory registration must take place not just upon sale of land but where there is a transfer by gift, by order of the court, disposition by assent or a legal mortgage by deposit of deeds: Land Registration Act 1925, s. 123 as amended. Despite the increase in the number of events which trigger compulsory registration some land will still be unregistered and the two systems will run in parallel for some time to come. If a transfer or disposition occurs, registration must be applied for within two months. Otherwise the legal title reverts to the original vendor or landlord. The purchaser of such land cannot give good title to a subsequent purchaser until he procures registration: *Pinekerry Ltd* v *Kenneth Needs (Contractors) Ltd* (1992) 64 P & CR 245. In practice the Land Registry will always accept an application for late registration. Legal charges must also be perfected by registration. As to the issue, status and content of land and charge certificates, see **1.4.2.3**.

Interests which are not registrable may be overriding or minor interests.

### 1.3.1.1 Overriding interests
These are listed in LRA 1925, s. 70(1). No interest falling outside this list can be an overriding one. Overriding interests bind purchasers, regardless of notice, even where

good consideration has been given. As a consequence, protection by registration is unnecessary. It is s. 70(1)(g) which gives rise to most problems: this protects the rights of every person in actual occupation of the land, unless that person failed to reveal their rights on enquiry being made. To obtain the benefit of the section, you must have both rights and be in actual occupation at the date of completion: see *Strand Securities Ltd* v *Caswell* [1965] Ch 958 and *Abbey National Building Society* v *Cann* [1991] 1 AC 56.

The relevant date for determining the existence of an overriding interest is the date of registration: *Abbey National* v *Cann.*

A purchaser can be protected if the purchase money is paid to two trustees: the overriding interest is overreached and is replaced by an interest in the proceeds of sale: *City of London Building Society* v *Flegg* [1988] AC 54.

**1.3.1.2    Minor interests**

These are all interests which are neither registered charges nor overriding interests. These interests must be entered on the register by way of notice, caution, restriction or inhibition, if they are to bind subsequent purchasers of the legal estate.

**1.3.1.3    Rectification**

Rectification of the land register is possible within certain limits. As to these, see **1.6.2.3**.

**1.3.2    UNREGISTERED LAND**

Under the system of unregistered conveyancing, the vendor proves his title to a potential purchaser, by reference to the title deeds and past conveyances. He must give evidence of 15 years of undisputed ownership. The protection of third-party rights in registered land depends partly on the doctrine of notice and partly on the operation of the Land Charges Act (LCA) 1972. Certain interests are classified by the Act as land charges. The law relating to the protection of such interests is confined to the statute. All other interests are governed by the pre-statutory rules: legal interests bind all, regardless of notice; the position with respect to equitable interests is still governed by the doctrine of notice.

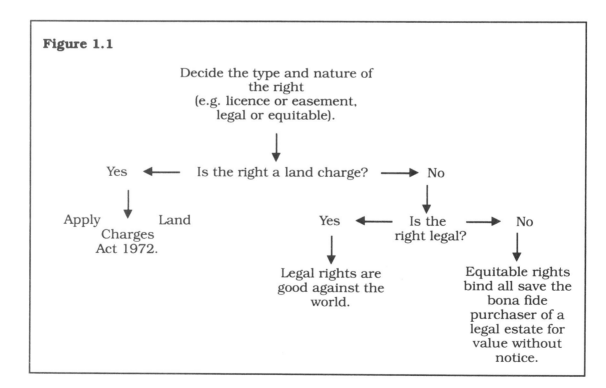

**Figure 1.1**

Decide the type and nature of the right (e.g. licence or easement, legal or equitable).

Is the right a land charge? — Yes / No

Yes → Apply Land Charges Act 1972.

No → Is the right legal? — Yes / No

Yes → Legal rights are good against the world.

No → Equitable rights bind all save the bona fide purchaser of a legal estate for value without notice.

### 1.3.2.1 Land charges

Important classes of land charge include:

| | |
|---|---|
| C(i) puisne mortgage | a legal mortgage where the mortgagee does not have the deeds |
| C(iii) general equitable charge | all equitable interests apart from rights of beneficiaries under a trust |
| C(iv) estate contracts | contracts to convey or create legal estates including options to purchase land |
| D(ii) restrictive covenants | |
| D(iii) equitable easements | includes equitable profits |

If the right is registrable and has been registered, it will bind everyone. The consequences of failure to register differ according to the class of the charge:

Classes C(i) and C(iii) do not bind a later purchaser of any estate or interest in land: LCA 1972, s. 4(5).

Classes C(iv) and D do not bind the purchaser of a legal interest for money or money's worth: LCA 1972, s. 4(6).

A purchaser does not have to give adequate consideration, and knowledge of the rights is irrelevant: *Midland Bank Trust Co. Ltd* v *Green* [1981] AC 513.

### 1.3.2.2 Interests not classified as land charges

If such an interest is a legal one, it will bind everyone regardless of notice. If the interest is an equitable one, it will bind all save the bona fide purchaser of the legal estate for value, without notice. Notice may be:

(a) actual;

(b) constructive (facts which would be revealed on proper and reasonable enquiries);

(c) imputed (an agent's knowledge is imputed to his principal).

Inquiries to be made for the purposes of avoiding constructive notice include:

(a) studying the deeds;

(b) inspecting the property and enquiring of residents as to any rights which they may have in it.

The doctrine of constructive notice means that a purchaser will be deemed to have notice of facts which would have come to light on proper enquiry, regardless of actual knowledge. A purchaser need only make such inspection as he ought reasonably to make: *Kingsnorth Finance Co. Ltd* v *Tizzard* [1986] 1 WLR 783.

# 1.4 Understanding the Documents

### 1.4.1 THE CONTRACT

For the statutory requirements as to form, see **1.2**. This section looks at the typical content of contracts for the sale of land. Generally the vendor is responsible for drafting the contract, since only the vendor knows exactly the extent of the land which is to be sold. Contracts usually consist of three distinct parts.

(a) The particulars of sale: the estate in and the physical extent of the land being sold. These may also list easements and covenants. Plans may be annexed depending on the nature of the plot being sold. Any errors in the particulars are likely to give the buyer a remedy in misrepresentation and/or misdescription.

(b)   The conditions of sale. These are divided into:

   (i)   General conditions, common to all transactions. Most sale contracts incorporate the Standard Conditions of Sale 1992 (referred to henceforth as 'the Standard Conditions').

   (ii)   Special conditions, terms peculiar to the transaction in issue. Typical examples cover:

      (1)   Latent incumbrances and defects in the buyer's title. Note the exception to the *caveat emptor* rule; the seller has a duty to disclose such matters.

      (2)   Occupants. Arguably there is a duty on the seller to disclose such occupants because their rights are incumbrances: *Williams and Glyn's Bank Ltd* v *Boland* [1981] AC 491.

      (3)   Overriding interests.

      (4)   The capacity in which the seller transfers the land.

   Most standard-form contracts will include a special condition stating that where there is a conflict between standard and special conditions the latter are to prevail.

(c)   The memorandum of agreement: the declaration that the seller wishes to sell and the buyer wishes to buy the property for a specified consideration.

## 1.4.2   PURCHASE DEEDS

Transfers of land can only be effected by deed: LPA 1925, s. 52. The deed is usually drafted by the purchaser; the vendor may attach a draft conveyance to the contract pursuant to his rights under LPA 1925, s. 48(1). The deed echoes the terms of the contract; its purpose is to put those terms into effect. The form of the deed is determined by whether the land is registered or unregistered. For unregistered land the deed is referred to as a conveyance; for registered land the deed is referred to as a Land Registry transfer. The term conveyance is frequently used to cover both types of transfer: see, for example, LPA 1925, s. 205(1)(ii). Because of the different statutory requirements of the two systems of conveyancing, the two types of deed will look very different.

### 1.4.2.1   Registered land — Land Registry transfer
For registered land, the form of the deed is determined by the Land Registration Rules 1925. A transfer of the whole of a property will follow the form of Land Registration Form 19.

*Commencement*
The deed will commence with a description of the property. A detailed description is not generally included, since the title number is sufficient to identify the property. If only part of a plot of land is to be sold, a more detailed description will be included. Generally such part transfers must include a plan which marks out the plot to be sold: Land Registration Rules 1925, r. 79. See **1.4.2.2**, *parcels clause*, for the status of such plans.

*The consideration and receipt clauses*
The consideration paid must be stated accurately or penalties are incurred under the Stamp Act 1891, s. 5. In property disputes, a record of valuable consideration often proves to be important, since it can affect title to the land. A receipt clause is sufficient evidence of receipt of the price. At common law, it was conclusive evidence. Equity now prevails, however, and evidence of non-payment is admissible.

*Covenants of title*
A vendor can convey as: beneficial owner; trustee or personal representative; settlor. These words import the title set out in s. 76 of and sch. 2 to the LPA 1925.

The Law of Property (Miscellaneous Provisions) Act 1994 provides for forms of covenants for title. It came into force on 1 July 1995.

*The words of grant*
These words actually pass the legal estate; the word *grant* need not be used: LPA 1925, s. 51. Form 19 uses the word *transfer*.

*Easements and covenants*
Those easements and covenants existing at the time of transfer are not generally listed since the transfer of the land covered by a specified title number includes all such rights and incumbrances: Land Registration Rules 1925, r. 251. Newly created easements or covenants will, however, be expressly included in the deed. These are particularly common where the vendor retains a proportion of the original plot of land.

## 1.4.2.2   Unregistered land — conveyance

The conveyance of unregistered land contains information similar to that of the Land Registry transfer, but looks entirely different. There is far more scope for variation, since most conveyances are individually drafted for the specific requirements of the property. Unlike the case of registered land, no form of wording is compulsory.

*Recital*
Recitals are compulsory only in certain situations and some modern conveyances omit them. There are three types:

(a)   narrative — explaining the immediate background to the vendor's title;

(b)   introductory — explaining the purpose of the conveyance, i.e., what the parties have agreed;

(c)   special — those required by statute, e.g., concerning personal representatives, trustees etc.

*Consideration and receipt clauses; words of grant*
The content and consequences of the terms are not markedly different from their equivalent in registered land (see **1.4.2.1**). Examples of the words of grant commonly used in conveyances include *convey* for freeholds and *demise* for leaseholds.

*Parcels clause*
This clause describes the land being granted. The land is often described by reference to a plan; if so, the plan must be mentioned in the conveyance in order to be incorporated into it. If the verbal description is unclear, however, a plan, which is physically part of the conveyance, can be looked at, even though not referred to in the conveyance: *Leachman* v *L and K Richardson Ltd* [1969] 1 WLR 1129. Any conflict between an incorporated plan and the verbal description will be resolved according to the particular construction of the document: see, for example, *Wallington* v *Townsend* [1939] Ch 588. It is a principle of construction that the boundaries marked on plans are general only. If the verbal description and/or the plan are unclear, extrinsic evidence of the surrounding circumstances is admissible and governs construction: *Willson* v *Greene* [1971] 1 WLR 635 at pp. 638–41. Extrinsic evidence cannot, however, be used to contradict the plain evidence of the conveyance: *Grigsby* v *Melville* [1974] 1 WLR 80, CA. It is rebuttably presumed that the conveyance includes everything down to the middle of the earth: *Grigsby* v *Melville*.

*Easements*
Any easements granted in the conveyance are introduced immediately after the parcels clause prefaced by the words TOGETHER WITH. The most common situation giving rise to such a clause is where the vendor retains some land and easements are created

over the retained land for the benefit of the alienated property. The conveyance will thus generally reveal only new easements granted; any subsisting prior to the conveyance pass automatically with the land unless specifically excluded by the deed: LPA 1925, s. 62.

*Exceptions and reservations*
These follow easements in the parcels clause and are prefaced by the words EXCEPT-ING AND RESERVING. An *exception* is any *existing* right or interest in existence at the date of the conveyance which is not to pass to the purchaser, for example mineral and mining rights. A *reservation* occurs where the vendor creates a *new* right for his benefit, e.g. a right to a rentcharge. Technically, a reservation, unlike an exception, operates as a grant by the purchaser back to the vendor. The distinction between the two used to be crucial: a further deed was required for a regrant (executed by the purchaser qua grantor). Such additional deeds are no longer necessary (LPA 1925, s. 65(1)) but the distinction is still material. The *contra proferentem* rule of construction requires grants to be construed against the grantor. Thus exceptions will be construed against the vendor and reservations against the purchaser: *St Edmundsbury Diocesan Board* v *Clark (No. 2)* [1975] 1 All ER 772.

*The habendum*
This names the grantee and limits the size of the estate transferred. A deed without a habendum is not a good root of title. Section 69 of LPA 1925 presumes the conveyance to pass the fee simple interest or other whole interest which the grantor has power to convey, unless a contrary intention appears. It is still necessary to state expressly what estate is to pass otherwise covenants for title are useless: *May* v *Platt* [1900] 1 Ch 616; *George Wimpey and Co. Ltd* v *Sohn* [1967] Ch 487 at p. 509.

*The 'subject to' clause*
This sets out the existing exceptions, reservations, restrictive covenants and other liabilities and incumbrances. Any express trusts, for example trusts stating that joint purchasers hold on trust for themselves as tenants in common or joint tenants beneficially as the case might be, may be set out in the habendum, or as a separate clause, or (if complex) in a separate document.

*Indemnity covenants*
These are often included. The vendor remains liable under many covenants, notwith-standing the fact that he has parted with the land. The purchaser therefore is generally expected to indemnify the vendor against an action for breach.

## 1.4.2.3 The land certificate and the charge certificate

The land certificate is a copy of the entry on the land register which is issued to the proprietor. It is not a document of title; the register itself is the true source of title. The certificate must, however, be produced on transfer of the land. If the property is subject to a mortgage, the Land Registry retain the land certificate and instead issue a charge certificate to the lender, the land certificate being reissued to the borrower when the loan is paid off. The Land Registry will issue copies of the register entries on request; these are referred to as *office copy entries*. The contents of both types of certificates are the same. They contain entries from the following registers.

*The property register*
This shows:

(a)  the estate in land which has been registered;

(b)  the physical extent of the plot of land, usually outlined in red on an annexed plan; other colour codings are used, e.g. for plots previously forming part of the relevant property but previously sold off; the plans are not conclusive as to the precise position of boundaries (Land Registration Rules 1925, r. 278);

(c)  any rights benefiting the land, such as covenants and easements;

(d)  cross-references to any superior or inferior titles such as freehold reversions, leases and subleases.

*The proprietorship register*
This shows:

    (a)   The class of title which is registered. The possible entries are:

        (i)    Title absolute. This is by far the most common entry and is as perfect a title as it is possible to have.

        (ii)   Possessory title. This has the same effect as title absolute except that the proprietor is subject to adverse interests existing at the date of first registration.

        (iii)  Qualified title. This is very rare and is used where there is an identified defect in title.

        (iv)  Good leasehold title. This is used where it has been impossible to verify the freehold reversionary interest, either because it is unregistered or where the registered freehold title is not absolute.

    (b)   The name and address of the proprietor.

    (c)   Restrictions on the proprietor's right to deal with the land such as the existence of a trust, the nature of the trust, or the identity of beneficiaries will not be included but a common example is where co-owners have indicated that they hold as tenants-in-common. Note that clearly not all trusts will be registered: see particularly the problems caused by co-ownership of the family home (see **5.2**).

*The charges register*
This shows incumbrances which, if substantial, may be listed in a schedule attached to the register, containing extracts from relevant documents of grant. Incumbrances include:

    (a)   easements;

    (b)   covenants which run with the land;

    (c)   registered minor interests (third-party rights);

    (d)   mortgages. One entry states the date on which the mortgage was created and the other contains the name and address of the mortgagee.

# 1.5    Special Cases

## 1.5.1    PERSONAL REPRESENTATIVES

### 1.5.1.1    Title to land
There are two types of personal representative: executors and administrators. The designation 'personal representative' covers both. All the deceased's property, whether personal or real, devolves on his personal representatives on death: Administration of Estates Act 1925, ss. 1–3.

Property vests in executors as a result of the operation of the will; title, therefore, passes prior to a grant of probate. The grant is, however, evidence of title. If an executor conveys land to a purchaser before probate, the conveyance is valid provided the will is ultimately proved: *Brazier* v *Hudson* (1836) 8 Sim 67. In practice, no purchaser will deal with an executor before probate is granted since it is probate which proves the will's validity and the appointment of executors. Probate is generally an administrative act by a clerk, but occasionally the will must be proved in court.

Administrators derive their title from the grant of letters of administration. Property vests in them only from the date of grant. For deaths after 1 July 1995 title vests in the

Public Trustee between death and grant: Law of Property (Miscellaneous Provisions) Act 1994. Previously title vested in the President of the Family Division: Administration of Estates Act (AEA) 1925, s. 9.

If a grant of representation to a personal representative is revoked, any previous conveyance to a purchaser remains valid: AEA 1925, s. 37. Section 7 of AEA 1925 provides that an executor of a sole or last surviving executor of a testator is the executor of that original testator; this devolution of office is conditional on each executor proving the relevant will. The chain of appointment is broken by:

(a) an intestacy;

(b) a failure of an executor to appoint an executor;

(c) a failure of an executor to take out probate.

### 1.5.1.2 Powers of personal representatives

Personal representatives have joint power over realty, rather than joint and several (as is the case with personalty). A personal representative who enters a contract for the sale of land will only bind the estate if acting with the authority of other personal representatives: *Fountain Forestry Ltd* v *Edwards* [1975] Ch 1. A sole or sole surviving personal representative can give a good receipt for purchase moneys, provided he is acting as such. All personal representatives must be parties to the conveyance or transfer. For transactions concluded after 1 July 1995 they will all have to join in the contract as well: Law of Property (Miscellaneous Provisions) Act 1994.

Personal representatives have wide powers to dispose of estates in land, including powers to sell, mortgage and lease property: AEA 1925, s. 39. Any such sale will overreach the beneficiaries' interests under the will or intestacy.

*Assent*

Personal representatives may dispose of land by assent: this is an additional means of passing a legal estate, available only to them. Its use for land is governed by AEA 1925 s. 36(1).

> *A personal representative may assent to the vesting, in any person who (whether by devise, bequest, devolution, appropriation or otherwise) may be entitled thereto, either beneficially or as trustee or personal representative, of any estate or interest in real estate to which the testator or intestate was entitled or over which he exercised a general power of appointment by his will, including the statutory power to dispose of entailed interests, and which devolved on the personal representative.*

An assent can only be used in favour of those:

(a) entitled under a will or intestacy (whether beneficially or as trustee);

(b) who take as a result of appropriation by personal representatives under AEA 1925, s. 41;

(c) who take under a deed of family arrangement.

This limitation of the use of assents depends on construing '*or otherwise*' *ejusdem generis* with the preceding words. If a wider construction is used, the section might cover almost any disposition by personal representatives, even a sale to a purchaser. In practice, assents are not used in respect of land sales by personal representatives.

*Problems encountered with respect to assents*

Only land to which the testator was entitled at the date of death can be passed by assent. If land passes to the estate after death, such land must be transferred by deed: *Re Stirrup's Contract* [1961] All ER 805.

Assents need to be in writing, signed by the personal representative and must name the assentee, to whom the property is to pass. No deed is required. These formal requirements apply even where the personal representative is the individual entitled under the will. A personal representative who is the sole beneficiary under the will must execute an assent in his own favour: *Re King's Will Trusts* [1964] Ch 542.

*Protection of the purchaser*
*Purchases from personal representatives* If personal representatives have previously assented to a beneficiary under a will or intestacy (as to which, see *Assent* above), AEA 1925, s. 36(6) provides protection for a subsequent purchaser. It provides that a statement in writing by the personal representatives, that they have not given or made a previous assent or conveyance, is sufficient evidence of that fact. Even if a previous assent or conveyance has taken place, the purchaser gets good title. The conveyance, to the purchaser, operates to divest any previous assentee of title, so long as notice of the previous assent was not endorsed on the grant of representation. A purchaser should therefore:

(a) check that there is no such endorsement;

(b) ensure that such a recital is included in the conveyance;

(c) ensure that the conveyance is endorsed on the grant of representation (a purchaser has a right so to insist under AEA 1925, s. 36(5)).

If the previous assentee sells the property to a third party, prior to the sale by the personal representatives and the consequent divesting of title, the third party gets good title: s. 36(6) provides no protection as regards such sales. Where land is registered, all that is necessary is a search of the register. If the personal representative is registered as the proprietor, the purchaser can rely on that alone. Any earlier assents would be on the register.

*Purchases from an assentee* The purchaser must check:

(a) the assent in favour of the assentee;

(b) the personal representatives' title, i.e. the grant of representation;

(c) that there are no endorsements on the grant of representation showing an assent of conveyance predating that to the vendor;

(d) that the assent to the vendor has been endorsed on the grant of representation.

Section 36(7) of AEA 1925 provides that an assent in favour of the legal estate is sufficient evidence that the assentee is entitled to the legal estate. It is not conclusive evidence. The purchaser has no protection where, for example, the assent itself shows that it is made in favour of the wrong person. In *Re Duce and Boots Cash Chemists (Southern) Ltd's Contract* [1937] Ch 642 the testator left a house to his son subject to a trust for his daughter to occupy it rent-free for life. An assent was exercised vesting the property in the son absolutely, but reciting the terms of the will. The assent had been wrongly made in the son's favour because the will made the daughter tenant for life under the Settled Land Act 1925. The purchaser could not get a good title, because of the recital.

## 1.5.2 TRUSTEES IN BANKRUPTCY

The following section outlines some important aspects of conveyancing transactions involving bankrupts and their trustees, where the relevant petition was presented or order made on or after 29 December 1986. Such transactions are governed by the Insolvency Act (IA) 1986 and the Insolvency Rules (IR) 1986. In the event of encountering earlier bankruptcies, reference should be made to the provisions of the Bankruptcy Act 1914, which governs such matters. Purchasers should also be alive to the potential problems of dealing with those on the edge of personal insolvency: the trustee and creditors have a number of powers to set aside improper transactions entered into in the years preceding bankruptcy proceedings. As to this see *Emmet on Title* at paragraphs 11.044–11.053 and generally *Muir Hunter on Personal Insolvency*.

### 1.5.2.1 Bankruptcy proceedings

Bankruptcy proceedings are initiated by petition. Such a petition may be issued by a creditor who is owed £750, or more, if the debtor appears either to be unable to pay or to have no prospect of paying: IA 1986, s. 267(2). The words 'presented', 'filed' or 'issued' tend to be used interchangeably for the initiation of proceedings. An unsatisfied execution of a court judgment or the failure to meet a statutory demand, served in the prescribed form, is sufficient evidence of such an inability to pay. The debtor may petition in his own bankruptcy, if unable to pay his debts: IA 1986, s. 272. The petition will then be heard by the court and a bankruptcy order may be made. The bankruptcy commences on the date of the order and continues until discharge: IA 1986, s. 278.

### 1.5.2.2 Land Registry entries

The Chief Land Registrar is notified, by the court, of the filing of a petition, which is then registered as a pending land action: IR 1986, rr. 6.13 and 6.43 and LCA 1972, s. 5(1)(b). The Registrar subsequently enters, on the proprietorship register, a creditor's notice against the title to any *registered* land likely to be affected: LRA 1925, s. 61(1); Land Registration Rules 1925, r. 179. This protects the rights of creditors until either a bankruptcy inhibition is registered, or the trustee in bankruptcy is registered as proprietor.

On the making of a bankruptcy order, the Official Receiver notifies the Chief Land Registrar; notice of the order is then entered on the register of writs and orders affecting land: IR 1986, r. 6.46(2) and LCA 1972, s. 6(1)(c). The Registrar then enters, on the proprietorship register, an inhibition against the title to any *registered* land likely to be affected by the bankruptcy: LRA 1925, s. 61(3) and Land Registration Rules 1925, r. 180. Until this inhibition is vacated, all dealings with the registered land are prevented, save for the registration of the trustee as proprietor.

### 1.5.2.3 Dealing with the property of the bankrupt

*Between the filing of the petition and the order*

Once a petition has been issued, any disposal of property by a bankrupt is void unless the transaction had the consent of the court, either at the time or on retrospective application: IA 1986, s. 284. Such transactions are valid, even if not so sanctioned, if no bankruptcy order is eventually made: s. 284(1). Once a petition is registered, any attempted conveyance by the bankrupt will be voidable unless entered into in good faith in respect of a contract entered into prior to registration. If the petition is not registered, a conveyance of the legal estate to a bona fide purchaser for value will be effective to pass title; a conveyance, in similar circumstances, of an equitable estate, will, however, be voidable, if the purchaser had actual or constructive notice of the petition. Once the order has been made and registered, no purported transfer by the bankrupt is binding on the trustee, whatever the circumstances: IA 1986, s. 284(4) and LCA 1972, ss. 5 and 6.

*Between the order and the appointment of a trustee in bankruptcy*

On the commencement of the bankruptcy, the Official Receiver automatically becomes the receiver and manager of the bankrupt's property: IA 1986, s. 287. As such he has no power to dispose of land owned forming part of the bankrupt's estate.

*Between the appointment of the trustee and the discharge of the bankruptcy*

On the appointment of a trustee in bankruptcy (who may or may not be the Official Receiver), the bankrupt's property vests automatically in the trustee, without the need for a conveyance: IA 1986, s. 306(2). Certain items of property are not automatically transferred. These include, pursuant to the Housing Act 1988, s. 117, assured tenancies, Rent Act protected tenancies and secure tenancies. Statutory tenancies are also excluded, since they consist of purely personal rights vested in the bankrupt as opposed to property in its strict sense. Vesting of title to the estate does not backdate the trustee's title to the start of the bankruptcy. For the position with the insolvent estates of deceased persons: see *Re Palmer* [1994] 3 All ER 835, CA.

In dealing with a trustee, in respect of *unregistered land*, a purchaser, therefore, will need to see proof of the trustee's appointment and authority to act. This should generally consist of certificates of appointment compiled pursuant to IR 1986, r. 6.120–122. They must, however, be endorsed with the date on which appointment took place since this is evidence of when vesting took place.

In dealing with a trustee, in respect of *registered land*, the trustee has the right, where the bankrupt was entitled both legally and beneficially to the land, to be registered as the proprietor: LRA 1925, s. 61(5). In these circumstances, the purchaser need only be concerned with the relevant entry on the register. If, prior to the registration of the trustee, a bona fide purchaser for value acquires the land and is registered as the proprietor, that purchaser will get good title against the trustee only if no creditor's notice or bankruptcy inhibition was previously registered.

A trustee in bankruptcy can give a good receipt for purchase money, since that trustee is designated a *trust corporation*: Law of Property (Amendment) Act 1926, s. 3. Payment to a trustee in bankruptcy is thus equivalent to payment to two trustees for the purposes of overreaching interests in land.

Particular care needs to be taken in respect of certain types of property. For mortgages, see **Chapter 4**.

*Trust property*
Property held by the bankrupt, on implied or express trust, does not pass to the trustee: IA 1986, s. 283(3)(a). In such a case, the trustee need not be a party to the conveyance. This is the case even where the bankrupt holds in trust for himself as well as others, though naturally the trustee is entitled in such circumstances to the bankrupt's beneficial interest. This situation is often encountered in respect of the ownership of the matrimonial home. When one of a number of persons who hold property upon trust for themselves (either as joint tenants or tenants in common) becomes bankrupt, that person may remain one of the trustees, even though his equitable interest will have passed to his trustee. The court does, however, have power to remove a bankrupt as trustee: Trustee Act 1925, ss. 41, 44 and 49. As to the position of the family home, see further **1.5.4** and **5.2**.

*Disclaimer*
A trustee in bankruptcy has power to disclaim any contract entered into by the bankrupt, prior to the petition, including one for the sale or purchase of land; the only grounds needed are that the trustee considers the contract an unprofitable one: IA 1986, s. 315. That right is not lost by taking possession of the property or doing other acts consistent with ownership. A vendor can, however, by giving notice under IA 1986, s. 316, compel a trustee to elect either to proceed or disclaim. Specific performance will not be ordered against a trustee, without the trustee's consent: *Pearce* v *Bastable's Trustee in Bankruptcy* [1910] 2 Ch 122. If, however, the trustee does disclaim or fail to pay the full purchase price, the vendor may keep any deposit paid: *Re Parnell* (1875) LR 10 Ch App 512.

*After-acquired property*
Property acquired by a bankrupt after the making of an order does not pass to the trustee unless the latter serves written notice that he or she wishes to claim the property: IA 1986, s. 307. The notice must be served within 48 days of the trustee becoming aware that the property has been acquired: IA 1986, s. 309(1)(a). Both before and after the service of such a notice, a bona fide purchaser for value of such property, who has no notice of the bankruptcy will get good title: IA 1986, s. 307(4).

*After the completion of bankruptcy proceedings*
On the completion of bankruptcy proceedings, either by discharge or annulment, the power to dispose of property reverts to the former bankrupt (except where the court

specifically orders otherwise): IA 1986, s. 280. The normal conveyancing rules then apply.

## 1.5.3    SETTLED LAND

The Trusts of Land and Appointment of Trustees Act 1996, s. 2, prohibits any new strict settlements being created. However, the Act will not apply to settlements already in existence. Strict settlements could be created by mistake. A notorious example is provided by the case of *Bannister* v *Bannister* [1948] 2 All ER 133 where the defendant conveyed her interest in two properties to her brother-in-law, the claimant, in exchange for the oral promise that she could live in one of the properties for the rest of her life. The conveyance did not include the oral promise and the claimant subsequently sought possession. The Court of Appeal held that the claimant was bound, by a constructive trust, to make good his oral promise. The trust created made the defendant a tenant for life within the meaning of the Settled Land Act (SLA) 1925. The key to a creation of a strict settlement is a succession of interests: SLA 1925, s. 1. Where someone is given a life interest or right to reside for life, such a settlement will be created. Accidental creation used to be common with, for example, home-made wills. In modern cases, the settlor will have no idea of the consequences of the arrangement. Sorting out the mess caused by such inadvertent drafting or disposition of property is likely to continue to be a feature of Chancery practice at all levels for some years to come. A case in point, *Costello* v *Costello* (1994) 70 P & CR 297, CA, concerned a council house purchased under the right to buy legislation.

Strict settlements are governed by the SLA 1925. For their effective operation strict settlements require two documents, a *trust instrument* and a *vesting instrument*: SLA 1925, s. 4(1). The former sets out the trusts in detail. They are thereby put *behind the curtain* for conveyancing purposes and need not concern the purchaser. The latter vests the legal estate in the appropriate person and gives the purchaser on a sale all necessary information. Where a settlement is created by will, the will itself is the trust instrument; the vesting instrument must be provided by an assent.

### 1.5.3.1    Ownership of settled land
Under SLA 1925, the legal estate is vested in the tenant for life. Where there is no tenant for life, both the legal estate and the statutory powers are vested in the *statutory owners*. Such owners may be specified in the instrument but in all other cases they are the SLA trustees: SLA 1925, s. 23. This occurs where:

(a)    a tenant for life is a minor;

(b)    no one is *entitled* to the income (a discretionary or accumulation trust); and

(c)    no one is entitled to *all* the income (e.g. one quarter to X and the rest to be accumulated).

The tenant for life has a dual capacity: he is a fiduciary of the owner of the legal estate and beneficial owner of his life interest.

### 1.5.3.2    Acquiring a good title to settled land
The only important function of SLA trustees is to give a valid receipt for capital moneys. The tenant for life has power to sell the settled land: SLA 1925, s. 38. The purchaser only obtains a good title if he pay his purchase moneys to two Settled Land Act trustees or a trust corporation: SLA 1925, ss. 18(1)(c) and 94(1). Payment to two trustees overreaches equitable interests. No sale can take place, however, until the two documents required for the creation of a strict settlement (as to which see **1.5.3**) have been executed: SLA 1925, s. 13. The Settled Land Act 1925, s. 18 vitiates any disposition unless the prescribed procedures are followed. Section 18 is neutralised by s. 102(5) and occasionally by s. 17 (see **1.5.3.6**). Until there is a vesting instrument, any purported disposition operates only as a contract for valuable consideration to carry out the transaction.

Section 13 will not vitiate:

(a) a disposition by the tenant for life of his *equitable* interest;

(b) a sale of the legal estate by the personal representatives;

(c) a disposition in favour of a bona fide purchaser of the legal estate for value without notice;

(d) any dispositions by the holder of the legal estate, if the land *ceases* to be settled land, before the vesting instrument is executed (s. 13 expressly applies only to settled land);

(e) a sale is made under the Law of Property (Amendment) Act 1926, s. 1.

On an *inter vivos* sale of settled land, the tenant for life must be a party, as the holder of the legal estate. The trustees of the settlement must be parties to receive the purchase moneys.

### 1.5.3.3 Sale by tenant for life

The tenant for life has, *inter alia*, the power of sale: SLA 1925, s. 38. The tenant for life's powers cannot be curtailed: SLA 1925, ss. 104, 106 and 108. They can, however, be increased. A provision that the powers can only be exercised with someone's consent is void, unless it relates to the disposition of the principal mansion house. The SLA 1925 requires the tenant for life to give the trustees notice for exercising the statutory powers; failure to do so does not, however, invalidate any disposition.

Under SLA 1925, s. 72, a conveyance by the tenant for life or statutory owner (for the meaning of which see **1.5.3.1**) overreaches:

(a) all estates, charges and interests arising under the settlement;

(b) limited owner's charges, general equitable charges and annuities, even if they predate settlement.

The owners of such interests have a claim against the purchase price.

A conveyance by a tenant for life or statutory owner, cannot overreach:

(a) a legal estate or legal mortgage existing at the date of the settlement;

(b) a legal mortgage created by the tenant for life to secure money already lent;

(c) a lease, easement or profit granted by the tenant for life under the statutory power;

(d) an estate contract, restrictive covenant or equitable easement.

### 1.5.3.4 Acquiring good title under the Settled Land Act 1925, s. 110(1)

Once a vesting instrument is executed, a conveyance on sale is void unless capital moneys are paid to two trustees or a trust corporation: SLA 1925, s. 18. The only exception is provided by SLA 1925, s. 110(1), which protects purchasers dealing in good faith with the tenant for life:

*On a sale, exchange, lease, mortgage, charge, or other disposition, a purchaser dealing in good faith with a tenant for life or statutory owner shall, as against all parties entitled under the settlement, be conclusively taken to have given the best price, consideration, or rent as the case may require, that could reasonably be obtained by the tenant for life or statutory owner, and to have complied with all the requisitions of this Act.*

'Requisitions', in this context, means requirements. Where a purchaser deals with a tenant for life, he obtains the protection of the section, even where he does not know

17

that he is dealing with a tenant for life: *Re Morgan's Lease* [1972] Ch 1 (but see *Weston v Henshaw* [1950] Ch 510 for a contrary view).

### 1.5.3.5 Purchaser's rights to see documents
The trusts of a settlement are behind the curtain and the purchaser has, with certain minor exceptions, no right to see them. The purchaser does have the right to see the vesting instrument: SLA 1925, s. 110(2).

### 1.5.3.6 Formerly settled land
An ordinary assent or conveyance of formerly settled land, not naming the Settled Land Act trustees, entitles the purchaser to assume that the assentee is absolutely and beneficially entitled: SLA 1925, s. 110(5). Where there is no such conveyance or assent, a deed of discharge is needed under SLA 1925, s. 17(3). This subsection provides that:

> *Where a deed or order of discharge contains no statement to the contrary a purchaser of a legal estate in the land to which the deed or order relates shall be entitled to assume that the land has ceased to be settled land. . . .*

In practice this happens in about 1% of cases.

### 1.5.3.7 Transfer of settled land
Transfers are seen by the Chief Land Registrar on the application to register the transfer. If the transfer (the vesting instrument) names the settlement trustees, the tenant for life (or statutory owner) would be registered as proprietor; a restriction will be placed on the register to the effect that no transfer by him is to be registered unless it complies with the SLA 1925, i.e. any capital moneys are paid to trustees or a trust corporation. Once the legal estate is later transferred by a transfer which is also a vesting instrument, or once a deed of discharge is executed, the restriction is removed.

### 1.5.4 TRUSTS OF LAND

Since 1 January 1997, when the Trusts of Land and Appointment of Trustees Act 1996 came into force, most land held for the benefit of more than one person is held under the new trusts of land regime.

Pre-existing strict settlements continue. It will still be possible to create an express trust for sale but s. 4(1) of the 1996 Act states:

> *In the case of every trust for sale of land created by a disposition there is to be implied, despite any provision to the contrary made by the disposition, a power for the trustees to postpone sale of the land; and the trustees are not liable in any way for postponing sale of the land, in the exercise of their discretion, for an indefinite period.*

The main differences between the trust of land and the trust for sale are that the interests are in land and not converted into an interest in the proceeds of any sale. There is not the same distinction between the duty to sell and the power to postpone as there was with trusts for sale — there are equal powers of postponement and sale.

### 1.5.4.1 Documents required
Trusts for sale were originally created by two documents, one setting out the trusts and the other effecting the conveyancing. This continues to be the practice with complicated trusts. Where the trusts are simple and short, a second document is unnecessary. Where there is a trust for sale under a will, the will is the trust instrument, but an assent is needed to pass the land to the trustees for sale. This is necessary even where the personal representatives and the trustees for sale are the same people: *Re King's Will Trusts* [1964] Ch 542.

Where two documents are used, all appointments of new trustees require two documents, one to appoint them to the trusts of the settlement or will and one to appoint them to the trusts of the property. Section 40 of the Trustee Act 1925 provides for the automatic vesting of the land in new trustees appointed by deed. Where the land is registered, s. 40 gives a right to have the Registrar give effect to the deed on the register of title: Land Registration Act 1925, s. 47.

An appointor must appoint the same persons as trustees for sale of the conveyance and of the trust for sale: LPA 1925, s. 24. This prevents any discrepancy arising. The purchaser is not concerned with any such discrepancy: LPA 1925, s. 24.

The 1996 Act amends LPA 1925, s. 24 so that it applies equally to the new trusts of land.

### 1.5.4.2 Powers of trustees of land

Under the 1996 Act trustees of land are given 'all the powers of an absolute owner' subject to their fiduciary duties and any express duties (ss. 6 and 8).

By s. 6(3) and (4) of the 1996 Act, trustees of land are given a specific power to purchase land:

> (a) by way of investment,
> (b) for occupation by any beneficiary, or
> (c) any other reason.

Sections 6(2) and 7 provide powers to partition and convey land to one or more beneficiaries subject to the consent of all the beneficiaries in trusts where the beneficaries are of full age and absolutely entitled to undivided shares in the property.

The powers under ss. 6 and 7 can be overridden or replaced by express provisions.

Section 9 gives trustees wide powers of delegation:

> (1) The trustees of land may, by power of attorney, delegate to any beneficiary or beneficiaries of full age and beneficially entitled to an interest in possession in land subject to the trust any of their functions as trustees which relate to the land.
> (2) Where trustees purport to delegate to a person by a power of attorney under subsection (1) functions relating to any land and another person in good faith deals with him in relation to the land, he shall be presumed in favour of that other person to have been a person to whom the functions could be delegated unless that other person has knowledge at the time of the transaction that he was not such a person.
> And it shall be conclusively presumed in favour of any purchaser whose interest depends on the validity of that transaction that that other person dealt in good faith and did not have such knowledge if that other person makes a statutory declaration to that effect before or within three months after the completion of the purchase.
> (3) A power of attorney under subsection (1) shall be given by all the trustees jointly and (unless expressed to be irrevocable and to be given by way of security) may be revoked by any one or more of them; and such a power is revoked by the appointment as a trustee of a person other than those by whom it is given (though not by any of those persons dying or otherwise ceasing to be a trustee).
> (4) Where a beneficiary to whom functions are delegated by a power of attorney under subsection (1) ceases to be a person beneficially entitled to an interest in possession in land subject to the trust—
> (a) if the functions are delegated to him alone, the power is revoked,
> (b) if the functions are delegated to him and to other beneficiaries to be exercised by them jointly (but not separately), the power is revoked if each of the other beneficiaries ceases to be so entitled (but otherwise functions exercisable in accordance with the power are so exercisable by the remaining beneficiary or beneficiaries), and
> (c) if the functions are delegated to him and to other beneficiaries to be exercised by them separately (or either separately or jointly), the power is revoked in so far as it relates to him.
> (5) A delegation under subsection (1) may be for any period or indefinite.
> (6) A power of attorney under subsection (1) cannot be an enduring power within the meaning of the Enduring Powers of Attorney Act 1985.

*(7)   Beneficiaries to whom functions have been delegated under subsection (1) are, in relation to the exercise of the functions, in the same position as trustees (with the same duties and liabilities); but such beneficiaries shall not be regarded as trustees for any other purposes (including, in particular, the purposes of any enactment permitting the delegation of functions by trustees or imposing requirements relating to the payment of capital money).*

*(8)   Where any function has been delegated to a beneficiary or beneficiaries under subsection (1), the trustees are jointly and severally liable for any act or default of the beneficiary, or any of the beneficiaries, in the exercise of the function if, and only if, the trustees did not exercise reasonable care in deciding to delegate the function to the beneficiary or beneficiaries.*

*(9)   Neither this section nor the repeal by this Act of section 29 of the Law of Property Act 1925 (which is superseded by this section) affects the operation after the commencement of this Act of any delegation effected before that commencement.*

Beneficiaries are given a new comprehensive right to be consulted and, with certain conditions, extended rights of occupation.

### Consultation with beneficiaries

*11.—(1)   The trustees of land shall in the exercise of any function relating to land subject to the trust—*

*(a)   so far as practicable, consult the beneficiaries of full age and beneficially entitled to an interest in possession in the land, and*

*(b)   so far as consistent with the general interest of the trust, give effect to the wishes of those beneficiaries, or (in case of dispute) of the majority (according to the value of their combined interests).*

*(2)   Subsection (1) does not apply—*

*(a)   in relation to a trust created by a disposition in so far as provision that it does not apply is made by the disposition,*

*(b)   in relation to a trust created or arising under a will made before the commencement of this Act, or*

*(c)   in relation to the exercise of the power mentioned in section 6(2).*

*(3)   Subsection (1) does not apply to a trust created before the commencement of this Act by a disposition, or a trust created after that commencement by reference to such a trust, unless provision to the effect that it is to apply is made by a deed executed—*

*(a)   in a case in which the trust was created by one person and he is of full capacity, by that person, or*

*(b)   in a case in which the trust was created by more than one person, by such of the persons who created the trust as are alive and of full capacity.*

*(4)   A deed executed for the purposes of subsection (3) is irrevocable.*

### Right of beneficiaries to occupy trust land

### The right to occupy

*12.—(1 )   A beneficiary who is beneficially entitled to an interest in possession in land subject to a trust of land is entitled by reason of his interest to occupy the land at any time if at that time—*

*(a)   the purposes of the trust include making the land available for his occupation (or for the occupation of beneficiaries of a class of which he is a member or of beneficiaries in general), or*

*(b)   the land is held by the trustees so as to be so available.*

*(2)   Subsection (1) does not confer on a beneficiary a right to occupy land if it is either unavailable or unsuitable for occupation by him.*

*(3)   This section is subject to section 13.*

### Exclusion and restriction of right to occupy

*13.—(1)   Where two or more beneficiaries are (or apart from this subsection would be) entitled under section 12 to occupy land, the trustees of land may exclude or restrict the entitlement of any one or more (but not all) of them.*

*(2)   Trustees may not under subsection (1)—*

(a)   unreasonably exclude any beneficiary's entitlement to occupy land, or

(b)   restrict any such entitlement to an unreasonable extent.

(3)   The trustees of land may from time to time impose reasonable conditions on any beneficiary in relation to his occupation of land by reason of his entitlement under section 12.

(4)   The matters to which trustees are to have regard in exercising the powers conferred by this section include—

(a)   the intentions of the person or persons (if any) who created the trust,

(b)   the purposes for which the land is held, and

(c)   the circumstances and wishes of each of the beneficiaries who is (or apart from any previous exercise by the trustees of those powers would be) entitled to occupy the land under section 12.

(5)   The conditions which may be imposed on a beneficiary under subsection (3) include, in particular, conditions requiring him—

(a)   to pay any outgoings or expenses in respect of the land, or

(b)   to assume any other obligation in relation to the land or to any activity which is or is proposed to be conducted there.

(6)   Where the entitlement of any beneficiary to occupy land under section 12 has been excluded or restricted, the conditions which may be imposed on any other beneficiary under subsection (3) include, in particular, conditions requiring him to—

(a)   make payments by way of compensation to the beneficiary whose entitlement has been excluded or restricted, or

(b)   forgo any payment or other benefit to which he would otherwise be entitled under the trust so as to benefit that beneficiary.

(7)   The powers conferred on trustees by this section may not be exercised—

(a)   so as prevent [sic] any person who is in occupation of land (whether or not by reason of an entitlement under section 12) from continuing to occupy the land, or

(b)   in a manner likely to result in any such person ceasing to occupy the land, unless he consents or the court has given approval.

(8)   The matters to which the court is to have regard in determining whether to give approval under subsection (7) include the matters mentioned in subsection (4)(a) to (c).

For applications for sale of land under the 1996 Act, see **5.4**.

### 1.5.4.3   Acquiring good title to land held under trusts for sale and trusts of land

The purchaser of land held on trust for sale gets a good title providing he pays the purchase moneys to at least two trustees or a trust corporation: LPA 1925, s. 27(2). This is the case whether or not he would otherwise have notice of interests under the trust, or be subject to overriding interests: *City of London Building Society* v *Flegg* [1988] AC 54. A bona fide purchaser for value without notice gets good title, even where the money is not paid to at least two trustees: *Caunce* v *Caunce* [1969] 1 WLR 286. However, in the case of registered land he will take subject to overriding interests. Where land has been subject to a trust for sale, but is no longer so, purchasers should check that the vendor is absolutely entitled; alternatively the purchaser could keep the trustees for sale in place to receive the purchase moneys: LPA 1925, ss. 23 and 27(1). This protects a purchaser where all the beneficiaries are of full age and entitled to call for the property.

Under the 1996 Act, LPA 1925, s. 27 will apply to the new trusts of land. In the case of unregistered land conveyances are not invalidated and therefore a purchaser would not be concerned with any contraventions of ss. 6, 7 and 11 unless he has actual knowledge (s. 16).

### 1.5.5   ADVERSE POSSESSION

Possession is evidence that the possessor is seised of a fee simple estate; such a possessor can only be ousted by someone with prior rights to the land. An owner can only bring an action if he does so within 12 years of being dispossessed: Limitation Act 1980, s. 15(1). After the lapse of 12 years a dispossessed owner's rights are therefore effectively extinguished and the possessor ('the squatter') acquires good title: this method of obtaining title is known as *adverse possession*. Such disputes are relatively common; they usually arise in boundary disputes, the land in question being on the border between plots of land belonging to claimant and defendant. There is fruitful scope for dispute since establishing possession and intent to possess are very much dependent on the particular facts of each case.

### 1.5.5.1 Requirements of adverse possession — the 12-year period

It is no longer necessary for the use made by the squatter to be inconsistent with that intended by the prior owner: *Buckinghamshire County Council* v *Moran* [1990] Ch 623. Where, however, the squatter uses the land in accordance with the intention of the prior owner, it will be more difficult to establish a case of adverse possession: *Pulleyn* v *Hall Aggregates (Thames Valley) Ltd* (1992) 65 P & CR 276, CA.

It is necessary to show both actual possession and intention to possess. The squatter must show clear and affirmative evidence, not only that they had the intention to possess, but that they made that intention clear to the world: *Pulleyn* v *Hall Aggregates* and *Wilson* v *Martin's Executors* [1993] 1 EGLR 178, CA. In the latter case, the mere walking round the disputed area woodland, collecting fallen timber for firewood and the mending of the boundary fences were held to be insufficient. But see *Hounslow LBC* v *Menchenben* [1997] NPC 40. These acts did not make it clear to the world at large that the squatter meant to *exclude* the owner from the property. An oral acknowledgment of the owner's title, during the 12-year-period does not necessarily interrupt adverse possession: *Browne* v *Perry* [1991] 1 WLR 1297, PC.

# 1.6 Remedies where Transfers Have Gone Wrong

The normal rules of contract apply to sales of land and the corresponding remedies are available. Some aspects typical of and/or peculiar to the sale of land are set out in this section. In all cases, primary and close attention must be given to the terms of the contract, including the Standard Conditions or other printed conditions.

On completion, the terms of the contract merge with those of the purchase deed. In so far as they cover the same ground, the terms of the deed replace those of the pre-existing contract. The parties may include a non-merger clause, however, which allows for the continued operation of the terms of the contract (see Standard Condition 7.4). In the absence of such a clause, an action cannot be maintained on the contract's provisions, but only on those of the purchase deed. However, actions on the contract may still be maintainable if they are not covered by the purchase deed: see for example *Hissett* v *Reading Roofing Co. Ltd* [1969] 1 WLR 1757.

Time of completion will be of the essence of the contract if:

(a) expressly so stated in the terms of the contract; or

(b) if made so by notice to complete; the period specified for completion by the notice to complete must be reasonable: *Behzadi* v *Shaftesbury Hotels Ltd* [1992] Ch 1, CA.

If time is of the essence, delay in completion will amount to a repudiatory breach; this gives the vendor the right to accept the breach and terminate the contract. Excessive delay may constitute evidence that the purchaser does not intend to complete and has thereby repudiated the contract. Thus, a vendor may be entitled to terminate, even in the absence of an express term or a notice that time is of the essence: *Graham* v *Pitkin* [1992] 1 WLR 403, PC. On the facts of the case, the delay was *not* such as to amount to a repudiation. In the absence of such a term and/or notice and/or delay amounting to a repudiation, delayed completion will amount to a breach of warranty, for which damages are payable, if loss is suffered as a result of the delay: *Raineri* v *Miles* [1981] AC 1050.

### 1.6.1 QUANTUM OF DAMAGES FOR FAILURE TO COMPLETE

The following section deals only with the modern position since the Law of Property (Miscellaneous Provisions) Act 1989 abolished the rule under *Bain* v *Fothergill* (1874)

LR 7 HL 158. The rule under *Bain* v *Fothergill* still applies to contracts which predate the Act: see, for example *Wards Construction (Medway)* v *Wajih* [1992] NPC 133.

The standard principles established in *Hadley* v *Baxendale* (1854) 9 Ex 341 apply in respect of sales of land. Loss caused by breach can be recovered if it:

    (a)  arises naturally from the breach, i.e. according to the usual course of events from the events in question; or

    (b)  may reasonably be supposed to have been in the contemplation of the parties when they made the contract, as a probable result of breach.

### 1.6.1.1   Expectation loss

Generally the quantum of consequential loss recoverable for breach of a contract to sell land is the difference between the contract price and the market price at the date of the breach. If the vendor resells, he may be entitled to the difference between the contract price and the price received on resale; he can also recover the expenses of the resale, provided the sale is soon enough after the breach to be attributable to it: *Noble* v *Edwardes* (1877) 5 ChD 378. Loss of development profit can be recovered if the defendant or his agent was aware of the development proposals at the time the contract was entered: *Cottril* v *Steyning and Littlehampton Building Society* [1966] 2 All ER 295. Even in cases of non-completion, the claimant can recover for damage caused by delay on the *Raineri* v *Miles* principle.

### 1.6.1.2   Reliance loss

It appears that reliance loss can be recovered *in addition* to expectation loss (in variance to general contract principles where a claimant would normally be expected to elect between recovering for his reliance and expectation loss and cannot recover both): *McGregor on Damages*, 15th edn., 1988; *Beard* v *Porter* [1948] 1 KB 321. Typical examples of reliance loss, in land transactions, include interest on mortgage or bridging finance, conveyancing costs wasted and those expended on purchasing a replacement property, charges for accommodation in the interim period and for furniture removal and storage. By electing to recover his reliance loss as an alternative to his expectation loss, a claimant can recover precontract expenses: see *McGregor*, para. 50; *Lloyd* v *Stanbury* [1971] 1 WLR 535.

Damages for mental distress are not available: such damages are available only where the contract is made specifically for the purpose of securing peace of mind for the claimant (a contract for provision of a holiday or leisure activities): *Hayes* v *James and Charles Dodd* [1990] 2 All ER 815.

A claimant must show that he has attempted to mitigate his loss; in the absence of some attempt to mitigate, damages may be discounted in the normal way. Mitigation will generally involve endeavouring to find a suitable replacement property or buyer (according to which party is in breach).

### 1.6.1.3   Misrepresentation

An actionable misrepresentation must be one of fact, communicated to the representee or to a class of which he is a member. The representee must have been induced by the representation to act in reliance on it. In the present context, the buyer may be able to prosecute an action for misrepresentation where, in reliance on a representation of fact, which turns out to be untrue, he enters the contract to purchase the property. A statement of opinion constitutes a representation that the seller holds the expressed opinion. If the buyer can establish that this was not the case, such a representation would be actionable: *Edgington* v *Fitzmaurice* (1885) 29 ChD 459. Where an actionable misrepresentation is established, a number of causes of action may be available. Two of the most important are described in the following paragraphs.

*Deceit*
This is a tortious action, for which it is necessary to prove that the seller acted fraudulently. This is a heavy onus to discharge and the allegation should not be

pleaded unless there are cogent grounds upon which to base the allegation. The remedy is rescission and/or damages. The measure of damages is tortious and is designed to place the claimant in the position in which he would have been had the representation not been made (rather than had the representation been true): *Doyle* v *Olby (Ironmongers) Ltd* [1969] 2 QB 158. All the damages flowing from the deceit are recoverable and are not limited to those which are reasonably foreseeable.

*Misrepresentation Act 1967, s. 2(1)*
The buyer need show only that:

(a)   the representation was false;

(b)   the transaction was entered in reliance on it; and

(c)   loss was thereby suffered.

This shifts the burden to the seller to show that he reasonably believed the representation to have been true. The remedy is damages or rescission. Damages are calculated using the same principles as for the tort of deceit: *Royscott Trust Ltd* v *Rogerson* [1991] 2 QB 297. The defence of contributory negligence is, in theory, available in respect of a misrepresentation claim under the 1967 Act, but in practice, it seems that it will rarely apply: *Gran Gelato Ltd* v *Richcliff (Group) Ltd* [1992] Ch 560.

### 1.6.1.4   Misdescription

This term is peculiar to land transactions and is not strictly a distinct species of misrepresentation, merely an application of the contractual principle. Misdescriptions are incorrect statements of fact concerning the property. If the property is wrongly described, for example in the particulars of sale, the land as promised is not that which is transferred; the vendor will, therefore, be in breach of contract. The description may concern, for example:

(a)   the physical extent of the land;

(b)   the nature of the interest transferred;

(c)   the nature of land.

If the misdescription is trivial, the purchaser may get virtually what he bargained for. In such cases, the appropriate remedy is nominal damages. If, however, the misdescription is a material one, the purchaser is allowed to seek specific performance of the contract with an abatement of the purchase price. If the misdescription is substantial, i.e. one that substantially deprives the purchaser of what he bargained for, he will be able to rescind the contract (see **1.6.2.4** for further detail).

### 1.6.1.5   Non-disclosure

The seller has a duty to disclose latent incumbrances or defects in his title. This is an exception to the normal *caveat emptor* principle. There is thus no duty to disclose patent or apparent defects, although the distinction is not always clear. The remedies available are similar to those for misdescription (see **1.6.1.4**). Where the effect of the non-disclosure is substantially to deprive the buyer of his bargain the court may rescind the contract. Failing this the court may order specific performance with a reduced purchase price. If the non-disclosure is trivial, only nominal damages will be available.

### 1.6.1.6   Deposits

A deposit is generally paid as a guarantee against breach: *Howe* v *Smith* (1884) 27 ChD 89; prima facie, therefore, the vendor should be able to retain it, if the purchaser defaults. Land contracts are a specific exception to the normal rule that such forfeiture provisions are penalties and thus ineffective. If the deposit demanded was unreasonably high, however, its retention will amount to a penalty and it must be refunded: *Workers Trust and Merchant Bank Ltd* v *Dojap Investments Ltd* [1993] AC 573. If the deposit is reasonable, the vendor may retain it, even in the absence of express contractual provision to that effect. Further, any part of the deposit which the purchaser failed to pay prior to his breach may be recoverable as damages: see *Emmet on Title*, para. 8.026; *Dewar* v *Mintoft* [1921] 2 KB 373. The court has, however, a statutory jurisdiction to order the return of the deposit under LPA 1925, s. 49(2). This discretion will not normally be exercised where the purchaser is in default: *Bidaisee* v *Sampath* [1995] NPC 59.

If a purchaser pays a deposit, but no binding contract is eventually entered into between the parties, the deposit must be refunded: *Chillingworth* v *Esche* [1924] 1 Ch 97.

## 1.6.2 EQUITABLE REMEDIES

The primary remedy for breach of a contract for the sale of land is damages. There are, however, a number of discretionary equitable remedies which may be available; in land transactions, the most important are specific performance, rectification and injunction. The general principles which govern the grant of such relief are applicable to land transfers. The claimant must show that damages would be an inadequate remedy and must persuade the court that there are grounds for the exercise of its discretion. The normal bars to the grant of equitable remedies apply:

(a) the doctrine of laches may bar relief if the claimant fails to request the relief within a reasonable time,

(b) the claimant must come to equity with clean hands: he must have fully performed currently accrued obligations under the contract and be ready and willing to perform future obligations. A trivial breach may be excused and the remedy granted: *Dyster* v *Randall* [1976] Ch 932. A person who was in breach of an essential condition will only be granted relief in the most exceptional circumstances: *Hedworth* v *Jenwise* [1994] EGCS 133, CA.

### 1.6.2.1 Specific performance

The remedy is not uncommon in land transactions: that no two properties are identical provides a strong argument in support of the submission that an award of damages would be inadequate: see *Eagleview Ltd* v *Worthgate Ltd* [1998] EGCS 119. Specific performance will not be granted, even where damages are shown to be inadequate, where: a bona fide purchaser for value has acquired an interest in the land, or the seller cannot give good title.

Where the court declines to grant specific performance, damages may be awarded in lieu, pursuant to the Supreme Court Act 1981, s. 50. The quantum of damages will be calculated according to the common law principles discussed at **1.6.1** to **1.6.2**. If an order of specific performance is made, but not complied with, the claimant may apply to the court for an award of damages: *Johnson* v *Agnew* [1980] AC 367.

### 1.6.2.2 Rectification

Rectification may be ordered where the buyer and seller have in fact agreed a particular term, but in error that term is wrongly set down or excluded from the document which purports to contain the contract between them.

On application for rectification, it must be established that both parties made the relevant mistake (the only exceptions to this requirement being where the omission or error is due to the defendant's fraud or where he would be acting unconscionably were he to resist rectification). Clear evidence must be adduced to obtain rectification; the standard of proof is high: see *Snell's Equity*, 29th edn., p. 632. The fact that the transaction makes no sense without the term in respect of which rectification is requested, may amount to sufficient grounds: see, for example, *Pigrem* v *Gaughran* [1993] NPC 9, CA. The court has jurisdiction to rectify both the contract and the conveyance. The court will not rectify a conveyance merely on the grounds that there has been confusion between the parties and solicitors acting for them as to what land should be included in the transfer: *Cambro Contractors Ltd* v *John Kenelly Sales Ltd* (1994) *The Times*, 14 April 1994, CA.

**1.6.2.3    Rectification of the land register**

Rectification of the land register is a related but distinct remedy. The principles governing the grant of rectification are set out in LRA 1925, s. 82. As a result of the operation of LRA 1925, s. 82(3), rectification cannot be ordered against a registered proprietor who is in possession unless:

(a)    the effect of the order is to give effect to an overriding interest or court order; or

(b)    the registered owner has fraudulently or negligently contributed towards the error; or

(c)    it would be unjust not to make the order against the registered proprietor.

If rectification is refused, the claimant may have an alternative remedy against the Chief Land Registrar under LRA 1925, s. 83 or an indemnity for loss suffered: see, for example, *Clark* v *Chief Land Registrar* [1994] Ch 370. The court has no power to grant rectification merely on the grounds that it would be just and equitable so to do: *Norwich and Peterborough Building Society* v *Steed* [1993] Ch 116.

**1.6.2.4    Rescission**

The effect of rescission is to set a transaction aside and to return a contracting party to the position he was in *prior* to entering the contract. Accounts are taken and property returned to its original owner; no damages will be payable, since these aim to put the parties back in the position in which they would have been had the contract been *performed*: see *Snell's Equity* at pp. 622–3 on the distinction between true rescission (referred to in this section) and rescission used in the context of termination in response to repudiatory breach. Rescission is not, technically, a judicial remedy, but is a right vested in a party in a number of circumstances. In land transactions common examples of such circumstances include:

(a)    fraudulent misrepresentation (see **1.6.1.3**);

(b)    innocent misrepresentation;

(c)    Misrepresentation Act 1967, s. 2(1) (see **1.6.1.3**);

(d)    constructive fraud, e.g. sales procured by undue influence;

(e)    express contractual provision, e.g. Standard Conditions 5.1 and 7.1; such clauses do not, however, give the vendor a right to rescind without showing some reasonable grounds for so doing (*Re Weston and Thomas's Contract* [1907] 1 Ch 412), but where time is of the essence and a purchaser defaults the courts will rarely allow the purchaser specific performance (*Union Eagle Ltd* v *Golden Achievement Ltd* [1997] AC 514 (10 minutes late);

(f)    mistake;

(g)    substantial misdescription of, or non-disclosure regarding, the property.

The right to rescind may be lost:

(a)    by acquiescence, where the party with the right to rescind chooses to affirm the contract, after the facts conferring the right have come to his notice;

(b)    where it is impossible to return the parties to their original positions;

(c)    where third parties have acquired rights in the property for valuable consideration.

**1.6.3**     **PROFESSIONAL NEGLIGENCE**

Where, for some reason, no sale is effected, the solicitor dealing with the transaction may have been negligent. Paradigm examples of such cases include failure to search correctly and/or adequately, with the result that the buyer does not obtain clear title. Note also, however, the wide-ranging scope of the duty of the solicitor; in *Mortgage Express Ltd* v *Bowerman and Partners* [1996] 2 All ER 836, for example, a solicitor who failed to warn a lender of a number of 'turns' in the sale of the property, was held to be liable. 'Turning' is a practice whereby a property is sold to associates or companies in the same group; prices are often inflated. The solicitor, acting for purchaser and lender, found out that the last truly open market sale had been at a considerably lower sum than the valuation. It was held that this fact should have been disclosed by the solicitor to the lender.

There is almost invariably a contractual nexus between the buyer and his solicitor but a tortious duty usually exists concurrently: *Henderson* v *Merrett Syndicates Ltd* [1995] 2 AC 145. A solicitor acting for a vendor does not owe a separate duty of care to the purchaser: *Gran Gelato Ltd* v *Richcliff (Group) Ltd* [1992] Ch 560. For the difficulties which arise for a solicitor acting for a buyer and lender: see *Bristol and West Building Society* v *Mothew* [1998] Ch 1.

The general principles of contractual damages apply. Where, for example, a solicitor negligently fails to discover an incumbrance on the property, the correct measure of damages is the difference between the price paid and the market value of the land subject to the restriction: *Ford* v *White and Co.* [1964] 1 WLR 885. In *G. and K. Ladenbau (UK) Ltd* v *Crawley and de Reya* [1978] 1 WLR 266, the court awarded damages additional to the normal measure: the claimants recovered a sum for consequential loss. The precise circumstances in which such an extra award will be made is not entirely clear: see *McGregor on Damages*, para. 1206.

An estate agent owes a duty in tort to a purchaser, in respect of negligent mis-statements, upon which the purchaser relied on entering a contract for the sale of land. An estate agent may be able to escape liability to a purchaser in respect of negligent misstatements upon which the purchaser relied on entering a contract for the sale of land by including a disclaimer. Such disclaimers can, subject to the precise circumstances, be held to be valid under the Unfair Contract Terms Act 1977, s. 11: *McCullagh* v *Lane Fox and Partners Ltd* [1996] 1 EGLR 35. However, estate agents and property developers may be guilty of a criminal offence, under the Property Misdescription Act 1992, if they misrepresent the state of the premises. Note that the Act does not apply to solicitors.

Several recent cases have concerned attempts to make surveyors liable for damages after a party entered into a purchase or loan on the basis of an allegedly negligent valuation. Remoteness of the loss claimed for and the difficulty of showing that the valuation was outside a 'band of reasonableness' makes it difficult for the claimant to succeed. See, for example, *Saddington* v *Colleys Professional Services* (1995) *The Times*, 22 June 1995, CA. Even where damages are awarded there may be a reduction for contributory negligence. For a comprehensive review of how such a deduction should be made: see *Platform Home Loans Ltd* v *Oyston Shipways Ltd and Others* [1999] 1 All ER 833, HL.

# TWO

# COVENANTS AND EASEMENTS

## 2.1 Introduction

Barristers of all years of call will often be asked to advise on the effects of particular terms (covenants) in title documents and in particular whether a covenant has survived a transfer of legal ownership of one or more of the affected properties. This chapter gives a guide to the main points to look for in dealing with problems relating to covenants. This is an area of some complexity and detailed research will usually be required. However, before consulting the practitioner texts such as *Preston and Newsome on Restrictive Covenants*, 8th edn., 1991, and *Woodfall on Landlord And Tenant* for leasehold covenants, it is particularly important to have a clear idea of what the relevant facts are and to try to apply the basic classifications outlined in this chapter to the facts.

## 2.2 Covenants Relating to Freehold Land

A covenant must be made by deed and will often, although not necessarily, be contained in the conveyance of the freehold estate to the covenantor. Between the original covenantor and covenantee all covenants are enforceable as a matter of contract. Where the ownership of one of the properties relating to a covenant changes, there will no longer be privity of contract as between the respective freeholders. At law the benefit of a covenant will, however, generally run, and in equity both the benefit and the burden may run with the freeholds.

### 2.2.1 ENFORCEMENT OF COVENANTS AT LAW

#### 2.2.1.1 Benefit of a covenant at law
The benefit of a covenant will run with the freehold of benefited land if the following rules are satisfied:

(a) the covenant must touch and concern the covenantee's land;

(b) at the time the covenant was made it must have been the intention of the parties that the covenant would run; under LPA 1925, s. 78 a covenant is deemed to have been made with the covenantee's successors in title and those deriving title under him;

(c) at the time the covenant was made the covenantee must have owned the legal estate in the benefited land;

(d) the claimant must derive his title from or under the original covenantee.

#### 2.2.1.2 Burden of a covenant at law
The burden will not normally run: *Rhone* v *Stephens* [1994] AC 310. However, where the burden of the covenant is related to a linked benefit the assignees of the covenantor may not take the benefit without also carrying the burden, e.g. a covenant to contribute

to the cost of maintenance of a private road where the covenantor is entitled to the use of the road: *Halsall* v *Brizell* [1957] Ch 169.

### 2.2.2 ENFORCEMENT OF COVENANTS IN EQUITY

In equity, a restrictive covenant may be enforceable as between successors in title subject to the rules derived from *Tulk* v *Moxhay* (1848) 2 Ph 774.

#### 2.2.2.1 Benefit of a covenant in equity
The successor in title to a covenantee will have the benefit of a covenant if:

(a)  the covenant is negative in substance, i.e. requires no expenditure by the covenantor or his successors;

(b)  the covenant touches and concerns the land of the covenantee;

(c)  the covenantee or his successor has retained land capable of benefiting from the covenant, and the covenant was made for the benefit of that land; and

(d)  the benefit of the covenant has passed to the covenantee's successor.

The benefit of the covenant may pass by one of three methods:

(a)  by express assignment at the time the benefited land was sold; or

(b)  by annexation to the benefited land; this should be done expressly, although if this has not been done to a post-1925 covenant, it has been held that under LPA 1925, s. 78(1) the covenant may be deemed to be annexed to the benefited land: *Federated Homes Ltd* v *Mill Lodge Properties Ltd* [1980] 1 WLR 594; or

(c)  under a building scheme. A building scheme will arise where a number of properties are sold under an identifiable scheme of development and the same covenants imposed on each purchaser with the intention that such covenants were to benefit mutually all the plots on the scheme: *Elliston* v *Reacher* [1908] 2 Ch 374; *Baxter* v *Four Oaks Properties Ltd* [1965] Ch 816; *Re Dolphin's Conveyance* [1970] Ch 654. A building scheme has other advantages since the covenant will attach to each plot and to every part of the plot automatically (*Brunner* v *Greenslade* [1971] Ch 993) and will endure even if two plots come into common ownership and are later divided again (*Texaco Antilles Ltd* v *Kernochan* [1973] AC 609).

#### 2.2.2.2 Burden of a covenant in equity
The burden of a covenant will run with land if:

(a)  the covenant is negative in substance;

(b)  at the date of the covenant the covenantee owned the land which was benefited by the covenant;

(c)  the original parties intended the burden to run with the land; this may be implied: LPA 1925, s. 79; and

(d)  the covenant was made post-1925, and the covenant was registered before the land was assigned, or that the assignee had notice of the covenant if it was created pre-1926.

### 2.2.3 DISCHARGE OF RESTRICTIVE COVENANTS

As a general rule a restrictive covenant will remain in force indefinitely, although it may be discharged in certain circumstances. Under LPA 1925, s. 84, the Lands Tribunal has the power to discharge or modify covenants on certain grounds, e.g. where changes in the neighbourhood have rendered the original covenant obsolete. On discharging a covenant, the Lands Tribunal has a discretion to order the party seeking the discharge to pay compensation to any party entitled to the benefit of the restriction. (See, for example, *Smith and Golding's Application* (1996) 71 P & CR 104 and *Re Milius's Application* (1995) 70 P & CR 427.)

The Housing Act 1985, s. 610, empowers the county court to discharge a covenant to enable a single dwelling to be divided into more than one dwelling.

A declaration may be granted in the Chancery Division of the High Court as to whether any land is subject to a particular restriction, or as to what effect, on its true construction, a particular restriction has.

### 2.2.4 REMEDIES FOR BREACH OF COVENANT

A court may award an injunction against the defendant to compel him to observe the covenant. If it would be oppressive to do so, or where the damage is limited and may be adequately compensated in money, the court may award damages instead. Injunctions may be prohibitory, requiring the covenantor to stop doing something (for example, using a dwellinghouse as a shop) or mandatory, requiring the covenantor to do something (for example, demolish a building). The courts are in general more willing to make a prohibitory order than a mandatory one.

## 2.3 Covenants Relating to Leaseholds

### 2.3.1 EXPRESS COVENANTS

Any lease will normally contain a number of covenants by both the landlord/reversioner and the tenant/leaseholder. Such covenants include covenants to pay rent, to insure the property, to keep the premises in good repair.

Where an express covenant not to assign, sub-let, or part with possession of the demised premises 'without the landlord's consent' is included, the landlord may not withhold that consent unreasonably, but must consent or refuse within a reasonable time and give reasons for his refusal: Landlord and Tenant Act 1927, s. 19(1)(a); Landlord and Tenant Act 1988, s. 1.

### 2.3.2 IMPLIED COVENANTS

A landlord impliedly covenants for quiet enjoyment and not to derogate from his grant. In certain circumstances there are implied covenants as to the habitability of the premises; see in particular the Landlord and Tenant Act 1985, ss. 11–14 (as amended by the Housing Act 1988).

Tenants usually (but not invariably) covenant to pay rent even if this is not expressed. Tenants impliedly covenant to pay rates and taxes. Implied covenants relating to the care of the premises vary according to the length of the term of the lease. A tenant holding a lease for a fixed term of years will be liable for all repairs for which his landlord is not expressly or impliedly responsible; a tenant on a short periodic lease will have no duty to keep the premises in repair other than to use the premises in a 'tenantlike' manner: *Warren* v *Keen* [1954] 1 QB 15.

### 2.3.3 USUAL COVENANTS

In the absence of express contrary agreement, it is an implied term of an equitable lease or a contract for a lease that the parties will undertake the 'usual covenants':

(a) tenant to pay the rent;

(b) tenant to pay the rates and taxes;

(c)  tenant to keep the premises in repair;

(d)  if the landlord expressly covenants to repair, tenant will allow reasonable access to view and repair;

(e)  landlord to allow quiet enjoyment;

(f)  landlord not to derogate from grant;

(g)  landlord to have right of re-entry for failure to pay rent (but not for breach of other covenants);

(h)  anything else usual in the trade, business or profession.

It is the usual practice to avoid these rules by attaching a full copy of the intended lease to the contract.

### 2.3.4  ENFORCEMENT OF LEASEHOLD COVENANTS UNDER THE LANDLORD AND TENANT (COVENANTS) ACT 1995

The Landlord and Tenant (Covenants) Act 1995 makes very important changes to this area of law but the most far-reaching provisions are not retrospective in effect. Therefore in dealing with a problem about enforceability of covenants the first question to determine is whether the lease was granted on or after 1 January 1996. This will not always be completely clear.

The definition of new tenancies to which the Act is to apply is given in s. 1(3)–(7):

> *(3)  For the purposes of this section a tenancy is a new tenancy if it is granted on or after the date on which this Act comes into force otherwise than in pursuance of—*
> *(a)  an agreement entered into before that date, or*
> *(b)  an order of a court made before that date.*
> *(4)  Subsection (3) has effect subject to section 20(1) in the case of overriding leases granted under section 19.*
> *(5)  Without prejudice to the generality of subsection (3), that subsection applies to the grant of a tenancy where by virtue of any variation of a tenancy there is a deemed surrender and regrant as it applies to any other grant of a tenancy.*
> *(6)  Where a tenancy granted on or after the date on which this Act comes into force is so granted in pursuance of an option granted before that date, the tenancy shall be regarded for the purposes of subsection (3) as granted in pursuance of an agreement entered into before that date (and accordingly is not a new tenancy), whether or not the option was exercised before that date.*
> *(7)  In subsection (6) 'option' includes right of first refusal.*

If the lease is one to which the Act applies the next question is whether the covenant is of a type governed by the Act. Section 2(1) provides the definition:

> *(1)  This Act applies to a landlord covenant or a tenant covenant of a tenancy—*
> *(a)  whether or not the covenant has reference to the subject matter of tenancy,* and
> *(b)  whether the covenant is express, implied or imposed by law,*
> *but does not apply to a covenant falling within subsection (2).*
> *(2)  Nothing in this Act affects any covenant imposed in pursuance of—*
> *(a)  section 35 or 155 of the Housing Act 1985 (covenants for repayment of discount on early disposals);*
> *(b)  paragraph 1 of Schedule 6A to that Act (covenants requiring redemption of landlord's share); or*
> *(c)  paragraph 1 or 3 of Schedule 2 to the Housing Associations Act 1985 (covenants for repaying of discount on early disposals or for restricting disposals).*

### 2.3.4.1  Transmission of covenants

If the Act applies to the lease and the covenant, the Act aims to provide a comprehensive formula to govern enforceability and transmission of covenants:

**3.**—(1)   *The benefit and burden of all landlord and tenant covenants of a tenancy—*

   *(a)   shall be annexed and incident to the whole, and to each and every part, of the premises demised by the tenancy and of the reversion in them, and*

   *(b)   shall in accordance with this section pass on an assignment of the whole or any part of those premises or of the reversion in them.*

   *(2)   Where the assignment is by the tenant under the tenancy then as from the assignment the assignee—*

   *(a)   becomes bound by the tenant covenants of the tenancy except to the extent that—*

      *(i)   immediately before the assignment they did not bind the assignor, or*

      *(ii)   they fall to be complied with in relation to any demised premises not comprised in the assignment; and*

   *(b)   becomes entitled to the benefit of the landlord covenants of the tenancy except to the extent that they fall to be complied with in relation to any such premises.*

   *(3)   Where the assignment is by the landlord under the tenancy, then as from the assignment the assignee—*

   *(a)   becomes bound by the landlord covenants of the tenancy except to the extent that—*

      *(i)   immediately before the assignment they did not bind the assignor, or*

      *(ii)   they fall to be complied with in relation to any demised premises not comprised in the assignment; and*

   *(b)   becomes entitled to the benefit of the tenant covenants or the tenancy except to the extent that they fall to be complied with in relation to any such premises.*

   *(4)   In determining for the purposes of subsection (2) or (3) whether any covenant bound the assignor immediately before the assignment, any waiver or release of the covenant which (in whatever terms) is expressed to be personal to the assignor shall be disregarded.*

   *(5)   Any landlord or tenant covenant of a tenancy which is restrictive of the user of land shall, as well as being capable of enforcement against an assignee, be capable of being enforced against any other person who is the owner or occupier of any demised premises to which the covenant relates, even though there is no express provision in the tenancy to that effect.*

   *(6)   Nothing in this section shall operate—*

   *(a)   in the case of a covenant which (in whatever terms) is expressed to be personal to any person, to make the covenant enforceable by or (as the case may be) against any other person; or*

   *(b)   to make a covenant enforceable against any person if, apart from this section, it would not be enforceable against him by reason of its not having been registered under the Land Registration Act 1925 or the Land Charges Act 1972.*

   *(7)   To the extent that there remains in force any rule of law by virtue of which the burden of a covenant whose subject matter is not in existence at the time when it is made does not run with the land affected unless the covenantor covenants on behalf of himself and his assigns, that rule of law is hereby abolished in relation to tenancies.*

The most important point is that, subject to limited exceptions and to a limited right of the parties to agree otherwise, the original tenant after assignment of the leasehold interest and the original landlord (subject to consent at the time) on the assignment of the reversion will not be liable for any subsequent breaches of covenants in the lease by the assignees. This is obviously of enormous practical importance where a subsequent assignee fails to pay rent or service charges and becomes insolvent. Under the old law a former lessee could be sued for an enormous amount of arrears despite not having been a tenant for many years and despite having no control whatsoever over the new tenants.

2.3.4.2   **Subject to agreement**
Given the potential financial significance of the issue the anti-avoidance provisions and the provision for a limited indemnity by agreement are likely to become of importance.

***Tenant guaranteeing performance of covenant by assignee***
**16.**—(1)   *Where on an assignment a tenant is to any extent released from a tenant covenant of a tenancy by virtue of this Act ('the relevant covenant'), nothing in this Act*

*(and in particular section 25) shall preclude him from entering into an authorised guarantee agreement with respect to the performance of that covenant by the assignee.*

*(2) For the purposes of this section an agreement is an authorised guarantee agreement if—*

*(a) under it the tenant guarantees the performance of the relevant covenant to any extent by the assignee; and*

*(b) it is entered into in the circumstances set out in subsection (3); and*

*(c) its provisions conform with subsections (4) and (5).*

*(3) Those circumstances are as follows—*

*(a) by virtue of a covenant against assignment (whether absolute or qualified) the assignment cannot be effected without the consent of the landlord under the tenancy or some other person;*

*(b) any such consent is given subject to a condition (lawfully imposed) that the tenant is to enter into an agreement guaranteeing the performance of the covenant by the assignee; and*

*(c) the agreement is entered into by the tenant in pursuance of that condition.*

*(4) An agreement is not an authorised guarantee agreement to the extent that it purports—*

*(a) to impose on the tenant any requirement to guarantee in any way the performance of the relevant covenant by any person other than the assignee; or*

*(b) to impose on the tenant any liability, restriction or other requirement (of whatever nature) in relation to any time after the assignee is released from that covenant by virtue of this Act.*

*(5) Subject to subsection (4), an authorised guarantee agreement may—*

*(a) impose on the tenant any liability as sole or principal debtor in respect of any obligation owed by the assignee under the relevant covenant;*

*(b) impose on the tenant liabilities as guarantor in respect of the assignee's performance of that covenant which are no more onerous than those to which he would be subject in the event of his being liable as sole or principal debtor in respect of any obligation owed by the assignee under that covenant;*

*(c) require the tenant, in the event of the tenancy assigned by him being disclaimed, to enter into a new tenancy of the premises comprised in the assignment—*

*(i) whose term expires not later than the term of the tenancy assigned by the tenant, and*

*(ii) whose tenant covenants are no more onerous than those of that tenancy;*

*(d) make provision incidental or supplementary to any provision made by virtue of any of paragraphs (a) to (c).*

*(6) Where a person ('the former tenant') is to any extent released from a covenant of a tenancy by virtue of section 11(2) as from an assignment and the assignor under the assignment enters into an authorised guarantee agreement with the landlord with respect to the performance of that covenant by the assignee under the assignment—*

*(a) the landlord may require the former tenant to enter into an agreement under which he guarantees, on terms corresponding to those of that authorised guarantee agreement, the performance of that covenant by the assignee under the assignment; and*

*(b) if its provisions conform with subsections (4) and (5), any such agreement shall be an authorised guarantee agreement for the purposes of this section; and*

*(c) in the application of this section in relation to any such agreement—*

*(i) subsections (2)(b) and (c) and (3) shall be omitted, and*

*(ii) any reference to the tenant or to the assignee shall be read as a reference to the former tenant or to the assignee under the assignment.*

*(7) For the purposes of subsection (1) it is immaterial that—*

*(a) the tenant has already made an authorised guarantee agreement in respect of a previous assignment by him of the tenancy referred to in that subsection, it having been subsequently revested in him following a disclaimer on behalf of the previous assignee, or*

*(b) the tenancy referred to in that subsection is a new tenancy entered into by the tenant in pursuance of an authorised guarantee agreement;*
*and in any such case subsections (2) to (5) shall apply accordingly.*

*(8) It is hereby declared that the rules of law relating to guarantees (and in particular those relating to the release of sureties) are, subject to its terms, applicable*

*in relation to any authorised guarantee agreement as in relation to any other guarantee agreement.*

### Agreement void if it restricts operation of the Act

**25.**—*(1) Any agreement relating to a tenancy is void to the extent that—*

*(a) it would apart from this section have effect to exclude, modify or otherwise frustrate the operation of any provision of this Act, or*

*(b) it provides for—*

*(i) the termination or surrender of the tenancy, or*

*(ii) the imposition on the tenant of any penalty, disability or liability,*

*in the event of the operation of any provision of this Act, or*

*(c) it provides for any of the matters referred to in paragraph (b)(i) or (ii) and does so (whether expressly or otherwise) in connection with, or in consequence of, the operation of any provision of this Act.*

*(2) To the extent that an agreement relating to a tenancy constitutes a covenant (whether absolute or qualified) against the assignment, or parting with the possession, of the premises demised by the tenancy or any part of them—*

*(a) the agreement is not void by virtue of subsection (1) by reason only of the fact that as such the covenant prohibits or restricts any such assignment or parting with possession; but*

*(b) paragraph (a) above does not otherwise affect the operation of that subsection in relation to the agreement (and in particular does not preclude its application to the agreement to the extent that it purports to regulate the giving of, or the making of any application for, consent to any such assignment or parting with possession).*

*(3) In accordance with section 16(1) nothing in this section applies to any agreement to the extent that it is an authorised guarantee agreement; but (without prejudice to the generality of subsection (1) above) an agreement is void to the extent that it is one falling within section 16(4)(a) or (b).*

A landlord seeking protection for the future may also seriously consider the circumstances in which assignment will be permitted to take place. Section 22 regulates the landlord's ability to withhold consent.

### Imposition of conditions regulating giving of landlord's consent to assignments

**22.** *After subsection (1) of section 19 of the Landlord and Tenant Act 1927 (provisions as to covenants not to assign etc. without licence or consent) there shall he inserted—*

*'(1A) Where the landlord and the tenant under a qualifying lease have entered into an agreement specifying for the purposes of this subsection—*

*(a) any circumstances in which the landlord may withhold his licence or consent to an assignment of the demised premises or any part of them, or*

*(b) any conditions subject to which any such licence or consent may be granted,*

*then the landlord—*

*(i) shall not be regarded as unreasonably witholding his licence or consent to any such assignment if he withholds it on the ground (and it is the case) that any such circumstances exist, and*

*(ii) if he gives such licence or consent subject to any such conditions shall not be regarded as giving it subject to unreasonable conditions;*

*and section 1 of the Landlord and Tenant Act 1988 (qualified duty to consent to assignment etc.) shall have effect subject to the provisions of this subsection.*

*(1B) Subsection (1A) of this section applies to such an agreement as is mentioned in that subsection—*

*(a) whether it is contained in the lease or not, and*

*(b) whether it is made at the time when the lease is granted or at any other time falling before the application for the landlord's licence or consent is made.*

*(1C) Subsection (1A) shall not, however, apply to any such agreement to the extent that any circumstances or conditions specified in it are framed by reference to any matter falling to be determined by the landlord or by any other person for the purposes of the agreement, unless under the terms of the agreement—*

*(a) that person's power to determine that matter is required to be exercised reasonably, or*

*(b) the tenant is given an unrestricted right to have any such determination reviewed by a person independent of both landlord and tenant whose identity is ascertainable by reference to the agreement,*

*and in the latter case the agreement provides for the determination made by any such independent person on the review to be conclusive as to the matter in question.*

*(1D) In its application to a qualifying lease, subsection (1)(b) of this section shall not have effect in relation to any assignment of the lease.*

*(1E) In subsections (1A) and (1D) of this section—*

*(a) 'qualifying lease' means any lease which is a new tenancy for the purposes of section 1 of the Landlord and Tenant (Covenants) Act 1995 other than a residential lease, namely a lease by which a building or part of a building is let wholly or mainly as a single private residence; and*

*(b) references to assignment include parting with possession on assignment.'*

## 2.3.5 ENFORCEMENT OF COVENANTS IN TENANCIES GRANTED BEFORE 1 JANUARY 1996

The position of tenants where the main provisions of the new Act do not apply is improved slightly by requirements that they are given notice by the landlord within six months of a default by an assignee and that they have the right on payment of the full sum due to have an intermediate lease granted to them so that they can take steps to get the assignee to comply with the covenants or in the event of further default obtain forfeiture of the assignee's lease. In other respects it is still necessary to apply the old rules about enforceability.

The general rule is that any covenant in a legal lease may be enforced as between the signatories of the lease, the original landlord and tenant, as there is privity of contract. Any covenant, which 'touches and concerns' the demised premises may be enforced as between the landlord or his assignees and the tenant or his assignees where there is privity of estate: *Spencer's Case* (1583) 5 Co Rep 16a.

### 2.3.5.1 The original landlord and tenant
Between the original signatories of the lease there is both privity of estate and of contract. The covenants contained in the lease may be enforced by either party according to general law of contract.

### 2.3.5.2 Landlord and tenant's assignee
Where a legal assignee of the tenant is in breach of a covenant, the landlord may either sue the assignee (privity of estate) or may sue the original tenant (privity of contract). The tenant is only liable for the term of the original lease. Thus, if a subsequent assignee breaches a covenant during a statutory extension of the assignee's term pursuant to the Landlord and Tenant Act 1954, the original tenant will not be held liable: *City of London Corporation v Fell* [1994] 1 AC 458. The landlord may also sue the tenant's assignee, and be sued by the assignee, where the covenants touch and concern the land; liability may only arise for breaches committed during the assignee's interest in the land.

### 2.3.5.3 Landlord's assignee and tenant
If the original landlord assigns his interest in the reversion, then the reversioner may enforce covenants against the tenant, and vice versa, so long as the covenants 'have reference to the subject matter of the lease' (LPA 1925, ss. 141(1) and 142(1)).

### 2.3.5.4 Landlord's assignee and tenant's assignee
The landlord's assignee bears the benefit and the burden of the covenants in the lease pursuant to LPA 1925, ss. 141(1) and 142(1), and the tenant's assignee does likewise pursuant to *Spencer's Case* (1583) 5 Co Rep 16a. The proviso that the covenant touches and concerns the land and the proviso that it must have reference to the subject matter of the lease have the same effect.

### 2.3.5.5 Landlord or landlord's assignees and sub-tenants
Where the tenant or his assignee creates a sub-tenancy, then there is neither privity of estate nor of contract as between the sub-tenant and the landlord or his assignee. The

sub-tenant may be restrained from breaching restrictive covenants under the rule in *Tulk* v *Moxhay* (1848) 2 Ph 774. It may be possible, if the right of re-entry has been reserved, for the landlord to re-enter the premises and bring about the forfeiture of the tenant's lease and therefore also the sub-tenant's sublease. Otherwise there is no direct method of direct enforcement as between the holder of the head lease and a sub-tenant.

### 2.3.6 REMEDIES FOR BREACH OF COVENANT

#### 2.3.6.1 Distraint

Distraint or distress is a common law remedy that entitles a landlord to seize goods found on the demised premises and sell them, using the proceeds to pay rent arrears owed by the tenant. The remedy may only be effected by the landlord or a court-appointed bailiff and is subject to common law and statutory restrictions.

#### 2.3.6.2 Damages

Damages may be claimed for breach of a covenant, other than for the non-payment of rent. In the event of a breach of covenant by the tenant, the measure of damages awarded to the landlord is the amount by which the value of the reversion is diminished by the breach. In the case of the landlord's breach, the tenant may recover the difference in the value of the demised property with the covenant performed, and with it not performed. In the case of a landlord's failure to undertake repairs in breach of a covenant, the tenant may also recover for damage to chattels caused by the want of repair, and for the cost of finding alternative accommodation, as well as for inconvenience and distress: *Calabar Properties Ltd* v *Stitcher* [1984] 1 WLR 287. If the claim is only for damages and it is commenced in the High Court, it should usually be started in the Queen's Bench Division.

#### 2.3.6.3 Injunction

An injunction may also be obtained, although the court is unlikely to grant an injunction restraining one of the parties from doing something that the party has already covenanted not to do. Under the Landlord and Tenant Act 1985, s. 17 the court can make an order for specific performance of a positive covenant, such as a covenant to repair.

#### 2.3.6.4 Forfeiture

Forfeiture is only available for breach of condition or if the lease expressly provides for forfeiture for breach of covenant.

Forfeiture may not be claimed if the breach has been waived, usually by the landlord or his agent accepting rent with knowledge of the breach.

If the covenant to pay rent is breached, a formal demand for rent should be made in the absence of a provision in the lease dispensing with such a demand. In fact every well-drawn lease includes such a term.

For other covenants a notice should be served pursuant to LPA 1925, s. 146. A section 146 notice should:

(a)  specify the breach;

(b)  give time for remedy if remediable; and

(c)  seek compensation (if required).

It appears that most breaches are now regarded as remediable and accordingly it is best to err on the side of caution: *Expert Clothing Service and Sales Ltd* v *Hillgate House Ltd* [1986] Ch 340. Breaches of a covenant not to assign or to sub-let are irremediable: *Scala House and District Property Co. Ltd* v *Forbes* [1974] QB 575.

The tenant is still entitled at the court's discretion under LPA 1925, s. 146(2) to relief from forfeiture. This can be granted even where the landlord has re-entered peaceably without a court order: *Billson* v *Residential Apartments Ltd* [1992] 1 AC 494.

If the forfeiture is based on the non-payment of rent, and the tenant is more than six months' rent in arrears, then he has an absolute right to relief under the Common Law Procedure Act 1852, ss. 210 and 212. If the arrears are of less than six months, the court may still grant relief on general equitable grounds.

If a head lease is forfeited then any sublease created from it would be automatically destroyed. However, the sub-tenant may also apply for relief under LPA 1925, s. 146(4) and, if granted relief, will become a direct tenant of the landlord upon such terms as the court thinks fit.

### 2.3.6.5 Claim for rent arrears

Proceedings for the recovery of rent arrears may be based on an express covenant to pay the rent, or implied by the reservation of rent. A maximum of six years' arrears may be claimed by the landlord: Limitation Act 1980, s. 19. Forfeiture may only be commenced in respect of rent arrears if payment is a condition of the lease or if there is a proviso for re-entry for non-payment.

A number of defences may be available to a claim to recover unpaid rent. First, if the term has been assigned, the original tenant is liable for the payment of rent throughout the whole term, but subsequent assignees are no longer liable once they have surrendered their interests. Secondly, on the assignment of the reversion, the tenant is not liable to the new landlord until he has been notified. Until such notice is received, payment to the old landlord will constitute valid discharge: LPA 1925, s. 151(1)(i). Thirdly, the landlord may not claim for the recovery of rent on premises that he knows have been used for immoral or illegal purposes: *Mason* v *Clarke* [1955] AC 778. Other defences include eviction, set-off against the landlord, payment of rent to a superior landlord, and denial of the landlord's title.

## 2.4 Easements

### 2.4.1 INTRODUCTION

Most of the easements which you will come across in practice are likely to fall within the well established categories such as rights of way and rights of support. There are, of course, interesting questions of degree and quality of use on the edges of these categories. If you can find no reported case which mirrors the fact situation with which you are dealing, it does not necessarily mean that it is impossible to establish that an easement exists. The courts do not regard the list of easements as closed and novel easements are recognised from time to time.

### 2.4.2 DEFINING PRINCIPLES

Certain principles can be derived from the case law to aid determination of the question whether an easement could exist in a particular situation. The most helpful starting point is still the definition by Danckwerts J in *Re Ellenborough Park* [1956] Ch 131:

(a) there must be a dominant and a servient tenement;

(b) an easement must accommodate the dominant tenement, that is be connected with its enjoyment and for its benefit;

(c) the dominant and servient owners must be different persons; and

(d) the right claimed must be capable of forming the subject matter of a grant.

Although an easement need not be created by deed, the nature of the right must be capable of exact definition, e.g., a right to a view may not subsist as an easement because that is not capable of definition: *William Aeldred's Case* (1610) 9 Co Rep 576; nor can there be an easement of privacy: *Chandler* v *Thompson* (1811) 3 Camp 80.

A right over land will not generally be recognised as an easement if it imposes a positive duty or necessitates expenditure by the servient owner: *Regis Property Co. Ltd* v *Redman* [1956] 2 QB 612. Although not strictly an easement, the courts have treated as such the obligation on a servient owner to fence his boundaries for the benefit of adjoining land: *Egerton* v *Harding* [1975] QB 62.

### 2.4.3 DISTINGUISHING EASEMENTS FROM OTHER RIGHTS

Easements can be confused with profits à prendre and public rights.

#### 2.4.3.1 Profits à prendre
A profit à prendre is the right to remove something from the land of another person, e.g., to cut wood or remove gravel. Like an easement it may exist as a legal or equitable interest in land. A profit à prendre does not, however, require a dominant tenement. The owner of a profit need not own any land to exercise his right.

#### 2.4.3.2 Public rights
Public rights may exist that are equivalent to either easements or profits à prendre, e.g., a public right of way. Public rights do not need to be appurtenant to a dominant tenement. Instead they may be enjoyed by the public at large, or, in the case of local customary rights, by the members of a certain parish: *Wyld* v *Silver* [1963] Ch 243.

## 2.5 Creation of Easements

An easement may either be legal or equitable. A legal easement must be for an interest equivalent to an estate in fee simple in possession or a term of years absolute: LPA 1925, s. 1(2). If it is created for any other period, e.g., for the lifetime of the dominant owner, then it will be equitable. Easements should normally be granted by deed (LPA 1925, s. 52), but other methods are recognised as outlined below.

### 2.5.1 EXPRESS GRANT OR RESERVATION

An easement is granted when the owner of the servient tenement confers the right on the dominant tenement. An easement is reserved when, for example, a landowner sells part of his land to another while retaining some right over the land he has sold for the benefit of his remaining land. The express grant or reservation of an easement should be executed by deed: LPA 1925, s. 52. In practice, the grant or reservation is often made in a deed of conveyance.

If the grant is over registered land there is a further requirement to create a legal easement: the grant must be registered in the form of entries on the titles to both the dominant and servient tenements. Until such registration is completed, the easement will remain in equity: Land Registration Act 1925, ss. 19 and 22. But note that subsisting legal easements constitute overriding interests under LPA 1925, s. 70(1).

### 2.5.2 IMPLIED GRANT

Easements may be implied into a grant for the benefit of a purchaser of land. An implied grant will be found either where it arises by necessity. For example, where a purchaser buys a parcel of land with no lawfully enforceable means of access, he may retain right of way over the vendor's adjoining land, or on the grounds of common intention: *Wong* v *Beaumont Property Trust Ltd* [1965] 1 QB 173.

### 2.5.3 THE RULE IN *WHEELDON* v *BURROWS*

An easement may also be implied into a grant following the rule in *Wheeldon* v *Burrows* (1879) 12 ChD 31. Where a landowner sells part of his land which had the benefit of a right capable of subsisting as an easement over the remaining part of his land (a quasi-easement), the purchaser will acquire with the land a legal easement provided that the right was:

(a) continuous and apparent;

(b) necessary to the reasonable enjoyment of the land; and

(c) in use at the time of the sale.

### 2.5.4 LAW OF PROPERTY ACT 1925, S. 62

Section 62 of the LPA 1925 provides that any 'conveyance of land' includes a wide range of items including all 'liberties, privileges, easements, rights and advantages whatsoever, appertaining or reputed to appertain to the land . . .' in the absence of any contrary intention. A 'conveyance' may include the grant of a lease although only if made in writing: LPA 1925, s. 205(1)(ii).

In *Wright* v *Macadam* [1949] 2 KB 744 a tenant was given permission by his landlord to store coal in a shed that did not form part of the demised premises. When a fresh lease was granted, the new grant was held to include the right to use the shed by virtue of LPA 1925, s. 62, and the right became a full legal easement. Accordingly, conveyances and leases often expressly exclude the effects of s. 62.

### 2.5.5 PRESCRIPTION

Legal easements may also be acquired by long use by means of one of three possible modes of prescription. The basis of the doctrine of prescription is the presumption of a grant at some time in the past which has since been lost. All three methods of prescription require that user is 'as of right' and that the benefit of the right claimed has been enjoyed during the period of use *nec vi, nec clam, nec precario*, i.e., without force, without secrecy, without permission. An easement acquired by prescription can only be obtained in perpetuity, and thus an easement can only be claimed by prescription by, or on behalf of, the fee simple of the dominant tenement as against the fee simple of the servient tenement.

### 2.5.6.1 Common law prescription

At common law, evidence of the use of a right for 20 years (living memory) will raise the presumption that the right has been enjoyed since time immemorial (1189) and is accordingly a legal right. This presumption can be rebutted (e.g., by showing that the dominant and servient tenements have been in common ownership at some date since 1189).

### 2.5.6.2 Prescription Act 1832

The Act distinguishes between a short period (20 years for easements and 30 years for profits à prendre) and a long period of user (40 years and 60 years respectively), save for the easement of the right to light, which is treated separately.

*The short period*
A claim under the short period merely assists a claim at common law by providing that such a claim cannot be defeated by evidence that the right must have arisen at some date since 1189. Such a claim may, however, be defeated in other ways (e.g., by showing that the right was used by permission).

*The long period*
After the long period the claim is indefeasible save if it is shown that the right was conferred at any time by written permission, or that, during the long period, the user was not as of right (e.g., oral permission was given during the period).

*Rights to light*
A claim to the right to light is indefeasible after 20 years except by evidence that it was enjoyed by express agreement or consent made in writing.

*Interruption*
A claim may be defeated by an interruption (which must be an adverse obstruction and not just mere non-user: *Smith* v *Baxter* [1900] 2 Ch 138, e.g., erection of a barrier over

a right of way); but only if the dominant owner submits to or acquiesces in the interruption for over a year after having notice of the interruption and of the identity of the interruptor.

*Rights of Light Act 1959, s. 2(1)*
Under this provision an 'interruption' to the dominant tenement's enjoyment of light may be caused by the registration in the local land charges register, in place of erecting a 'spite fence'.

Sections 7 and 8 of the Prescription Act 1832 provide for certain circumstances when deductions should be made from the period relied upon (e.g., any part of the period during which the fee simple owner of the dominant tenement was a minor). These rules are complex and should be studied before advising.

Under the Prescription Act 1832 the period relied upon must be 'next before some suit or action'. Past use which has ceased cannot be relied upon.

**2.5.6.3    Lost modern grant**
This method of prescribing is a legal fiction based on the presumption that if user as of right has been enjoyed for 20 years, the right must have been granted by a deed that has since been lost. The presumption may be rebutted by proving either that no grant was in fact made, or that no servient owner could have lawfully made the grant during the time it is alleged to have been made. The advantage of this method over that of the Prescription Act 1832 is that the 20 years' user need be neither continuous nor that period immediately preceding the action: *Tehidy Minerals Ltd* v *Norman* [1971] 2 QB 528.

**2.5.7    ACCESS TO NEIGHBOURING LAND ACT 1992**

Under this Act, a person who wishes to gain access to neighbouring land, the servient tenement, for the purpose of carrying out works to his own land, the dominant tenement, and needs permission to do so but cannot obtain it, may apply to the court for an 'access order'. Such an application should be commenced in the county court and is governed by the provisions of the Civil Procedure Rules (CPR) 1998, sch. 2 which preserves CCR O. 49.

Under s. 1(3)(a) and (b) of the 1992 Act the court will refuse an order if it is satisfied that either the respondent or anyone else would suffer interference or disturbance to the enjoyment of their land, or if the respondent or any other person in occupation would suffer undue hardship, so (in either case) as to make the order unreasonable.

If the order is registered either under the LCA 1972, s. 6(1)(d) or as a notice under the LRA 1925, s. 49(1)(j), the successors in title to the servient tenement, and anyone who derives a title from that estate after the making of the order, are required to allow the applicant to do anything that he is permitted to do under the order. The right of access conferred by the Act is not, however, intended to be of a permanent nature.

**2.5.8    PARTY WALL ETC. ACT 1996**

This Act, which came into force on 1 July 1997, gives new rights and obligations to landowners. Where there is no building or structure on a boundary, a landowner may build a party wall or a wall on his own side of the boundary. If there is an existing party wall, the landowner is given new rights and obligations in respect of repairs and maintenance. It expressly states that these rights are separate from easements and do not alter the position on any existing easement nor do they constitute a new easement (s. 9).

Any adjoining occupiers have to be given notice in accordance with the provisions of ss. 1, 3 and 6 of the Act. A dispute resolution procedure is provided by s. 10 and there is provision for compensation for adjoining occupiers for damage caused to their property in exercise of the rights under the Act.

## 2.6 Extinction of Easements

Once it has been decided that an easement had been created, it is always important to check it has not been extinguished.

### 2.6.1 STATUTE

Easements may be extinguished by statute, e.g., Commons Registration Act 1965 defining 'common land', Housing Act 1985 dealing with easements over land compulsorily purchased by local authorities.

### 2.6.2 EXPRESS RELEASE

A legal easement can only be expressly released by deed. An equitable easement may be lost by agreement backed by consideration, or by acquiescence and consent from which it would be inequitable to resile: *Davies* v *Marshall* (1816) 10 CB NS 697.

### 2.6.3 IMPLIED RELEASE

An easement may be extinguished by actual abandonment of the right. Abandonment is only constituted by non-user of the right combined with a clear intention to abandon it. Non-user alone is not sufficient to raise the presumption of abandonment even where there has been non-user over a very long period: *Benn* v *Harding* (1992) *The Times*, 13 October 1992 (non-user of a right of way for 175 years).

### 2.6.4 UNITY OF POSSESSION

Ownership with entitlement to possession of both the servient and the dominant tenements simultaneously extinguishes any easements. Unity of possession alone will only suspend an easement, while an easement will continue if there is unity of ownership but not of possession.

## 2.7 Remedies for the Disturbance of Easements

### 2.7.1 ABATEMENT

Where the enjoyment of an easement is obstructed the owner of the dominant tenement may enter the servient tenement and remove the obstruction. The law does not, however, favour abatement even where the act of obstruction does amount to a nuisance: *Lagan Navigation Co.* v *Lambeg Bleaching, Dyeing & Finishing Co.* [1927] AC 226.

### 2.7.2 CLAIM

The more usual course is to commence a claim for nuisance. The party in possession of the dominant tenement should sue; the landlord, or reversioner may be entitled to sue even if not in possession if the obstruction is of a permanent nature likely to affect the value of the reversion, or if it is affecting the reversioner's present rights, e.g., the tenants are refusing to pay rent as a result of the obstruction. The party causing the disturbance should be the defendant to the proceedings.

In a claim the party seeking to enforce their right under the easement must show how the easement arose. It is possible to plead more than one method, e.g., by prescription and lost modern grant. An action for disturbance may also be used as a defence to a claim against the dominant owner for trespass or nuisance.

#### 2.7.2.1 Remedies

If the disturbance of the easement was a one-off occurrence then the correct remedy to claim is for damages at common law. If the disturbance is continuous then an injunction should be sought. The court may award an injunction if, in all the circumstances, it considers it to be just and equitable. A *quia timet* injunction may be sought, but it is necessary to show that unless it is granted damage will result: *Leeds Industrial Co-operative Society Ltd* v *Slack* [1924] AC 851. It is possible to get a declaration that an injunction could not be obtained in the future for the alleged interference with a right of way but it is likely to be appropriate only in rare cases: *Greenwich Health Care NHS Trust* v *London Quadrant Housing Trust* (1998) *The Times*, 11 June 1998.

### 2.7.2.2 Claims relating to profits à prendre

While the owner of an easement cannot maintain a claim for trespass for the disturbance of the easement, but only one for nuisance, the owner of a 'several profit' (i.e. the exclusive right to remove something from another's land) may bring a claim for trespass or nuisance. Proceedings for trespass may still be maintained even if no loss is suffered; someone fishing a river over which there is a several profit may be liable for trespass even if he catches no fish: *Patrick* v *Greenway* (1796) 1 Wms Saund 346n. A person entitled to a 'profit in common' (a right shared with others) may only bring a claim for nuisance.

# 2.8 Disputing the Assertion of an Easement

Where a party to a claim is claiming damages for the disturbance of an easement or profit, the other party may dispute the assertion of the right's subsistence. Bringing a claim for trespass against someone exercising a purported easement will have the same effect.

If the existence of an easement is admitted, a servient owner may still commence a claim for nuisance or trespass against the party exercising the easement on the grounds that unlawful damage is being caused by the user, or that the right is being used beyond the extent to which the dominant owner is entitled.

# THREE

# NEIGHBOUR DISPUTES

## 3.1 Generally

Disputes between neighbours often involve consideration of aspects of all the areas discussed so far. Boundary disputes usually take the form of a claim in trespass. Factually what has most frequently happened is that a landowner has either pulled down a boundary structure, erected a new one or built a part of a building along a boundary of his property in such a way that the neighbour claims it encroaches on his or her land. Disputes about rights of way or other rights of access and use of a neighbour's land can of course arise separately but often they are part of a boundary dispute.

## 3.2 Subject Matter

The recently qualified barrister will usually be concerned with disputes between owners of dwelling houses or perhaps small commercial properties. However, such disputes can occur in relation to commercial or industrial properties, for example *Wigginton and Milner Ltd* v *Winster Engineering Ltd* [1978] 1 WLR 1462.

In social and human terms, neighbour disputes are often very bitter and the cost and effort involved in them is out of all proportion to the value of the subject matter which may only involve ownership of a strip of suburdan garden measuring 15 metres by 45 centimetres, or an easement of a right of way over a corner of a field. Because of the personal element involved these cases are often very difficult to settle. Each side feels affronted at the thought of giving in to the other side and rapidly the question of who pays the costs incurred so far becomes far more important than the original issue.

Although the subject matter of these disputes is often of little value, you should always be aware that sometimes a very small piece of land will have a strategic value, particularly ransom strips taken to prevent other developers from gaining advantage from access roads etc. that a developer has put in to service its development. Equally a neighbour's right of way over the corner of a garden may mean that owners cannot satisfy council requirements for provision of access or parking and so be unable to obtain planning permission to develop their land.

## 3.3 Forum

Although the subject matter frequently involves points of a Chancery type, most neighbour disputes are tried in the county court. This means that they may well be heard by a circuit judge or recorder without any Chancery or conveyancing experience. Counsel has to be ready to explain the law and the issues fully. County courts, being local, carry with them the advantage that the judge can be asked, if appropriate, to view the site. Because of the time and costs involved this is less likely in a High Court action.

## 3.4 Probable Issues

The dispute often arises because the conveyancing documents are either inconsistent with each other or less than clear. It can sometimes also happen that these documents do not relate to the real situation on the ground. This is a common occurrence in the development of estates where the plots are laid out by the builders and surveyors in a different way from the plots shown on the plans given to the developer's solicitors. Sometimes also the plans can be clear but there have been encroachments of very long standing. In relation to such encroachments and purported easements, neighbours who had been on friendly terms are most unlikely to have given any thought to the legal status of any arrangement and many years later it is very hard to fathom what was intended.

### 3.4.1 POSITION OF BOUNDARY

If the position of the boundary is in issue then it is important to work out how title has been derived (see **Chapter 1**) paying particular attention to matters such as:

(a) the status of the conveyancing plan;

(b) inconsistency between the parcels clause and the plan;

(c) whether the two plots were ever in common ownership. If they were, the earlier conveyance must prevail since when the vendor executed the later conveyance he could not convey land already conveyed by the first conveyance;

(d) where (when the deeds do not help) the historic boundaries of the properties were (this issue can arise years after those boundaries have been removed or destroyed);

(e) if any of the plans or parcels clauses were by reference to measurements, where those measurements ought to be taken from;

(f) whether the 'hedge and ditch' rule applies (see *Allen Wilberley Building Ltd* v *Insley* [1997] 2 All ER 897, HL);

(g) whether the conveyance was by reference to a parcel on the Ordnance Survey and if so whether the relevant boundary structure (at the time of the survey) was a hedge. The rule in those cases is that the mid-line of the hedge is the boundary (see *Davey* v *Harrow Corporation* [1958] 1 QB 60 and *Hall* v *Dorling* [1996] EGCS 58, CA);

(h) whether the party who has 'encroached' has done so for sufficiently long and in such circumstances as to enable him to have acquired the disputed land by adverse possession (see **1.5.5**).

## 3.5 Evidence

### 3.5.1 'OLDEST INHABITANT' EVIDENCE

Although the case may turn to an extent on the construction of the conveyances, experience shows that: (i) many conveyances are too vaguely drawn and the plans on them too small to be of much assistance in themselves; and therefore (ii) there is often a need for 'oldest inhabitant' evidence as to where boundary structures formerly stood. However, if the parcels clause is clear no other extrinsic evidence will be admitted: *Woolls* v *Parling* (1999), *The Times*, 9 March 1999, CA.

If 'oldest inhabitant' evidence is likely to be necessary it should be borne in mind that such witnesses are often elderly and infirm and could die before the hearing, or be incapable of being present on the day. Care needs therefore to be taken in the early stages of the case to see that every step is taken to preserve this evidence in a form which the court of trial can receive.

### 3.5.2    SURVEYORS

In many cases the evidence of a surveyor is necessary to plot out on a suitable plan the effect of one side's case, including an interpretation on the ground of the conveyance plan and/or parcels clause. Evidence of this kind (and any other 'visual aid') is of great assistance to the judge.

### 3.5.3    SITE VISIT

It is quite common for the judge to be asked to view the site during the course of the trial.

## 3.6    Procedure

Almost invariably boundary disputes will not be commenced using the new CPR, Part 7 procedure. In old cases you will see proceedings commenced by a writ in the High Court or a particulars of claim in the county court. Occasionally, if the only issue was construction, proceedings would have been commenced by an originating summons and would now be started using the new CPR Part 8 procedure. Even with new fast track procedures, disclosure and an expert report will be necessary and often an application for an interim injunction will be sought. All this tends to make this type of litigation much more expensive than (in many cases) the subject matter merits.

## 3.7    Registered Land

### 3.7.1    ISSUES INVOLVED

With the growth and continued expansion of the system of land registration, neighbour disputes and their resolution will involve questions of rectification of the register of title. It is rare for the register to contain a properly surveyed boundary (it can be done but is expensive). Therefore the entry on the register can be no better than the conveyancing documents (often dating back to pre-registration instruments) on which it is based.

### 3.7.2    RECTIFICATION OF THE REGISTER

The court has a general power to rectify the register of title and will readily do so to give effect to a judgment. Thus if it appears that the boundary is wrongly shown on the register, the court will order the register to be rectified. But it is not always necessary to do this. The registry plan is usually of small scale with a thick boundary line and can do no more than indicate the general area of the boundaries. It is probably correct so far as it goes. The dispute (likely often only to affect less than a metre) is a matter of finer detail than the plan can show.

### 3.7.3    WHEN RECTIFICATION OF IMPORTANCE

One area where rectification can be very important (and difficult) is where the developer has laid out the plots differently on the ground from those shown in the conveyancing documents. Each case will turn on its own facts but it is easy to envisage (i) cases where the registered title is correctly shown and the plotting on the ground is wrong and (ii) cases where the vendor cannot have sold (because of earlier sales) the land which he has purported to transfer.

### 3.7.4    MISTAKES

Sometimes the problem over the boundary can arise because there has been a mistake on a plan or some other document filed in the registry. If the registered proprietor has suffered loss because of this error, then (unless it is the result of the fraud or lack of proper care of himself or his predecessor) he is entitled to claim statutory indemnity from the registry. In many cases the amount of the indemnity is not adequate.

The summary given here is very short, the subject is complex and reference should be made to the Land Registration Act 1925, s. 83 and to specialist textbooks on conveyancing and registered land. While it is a topic that has to be considered when advising on boundary disputes, it is not particularly common in practice.

## 3.8    Example of a Boundary Dispute

The following is an example of a boundary dispute being fought out in the county court. Typically a brief in such a case would also include a large and generally unhelpful selection of increasingly acrimonious correspondence between the protagonists. There would also probably be more plans from various sources and sometimes old (and often handwritten) conveyances. For reasons of space we have omitted most of the plans and conveyances as well as the correspondence.

We have also not included any photographs but there are usually quite a number of these as well. Some of those provided by the clients can be helpful in establishing certain things from a historical basis, for example, whether a building was on the site at a particular time or whether there was a hedge or fence. But they are much less instructive if the purpose is to try to establish usage. In this example case the photographs would be mostly of bicycles lying around and children playing. Photographs taken by the expert witnesses for either side or the parties of the site as it is at present do not have much evidential value usually but are very useful in setting the scene for the judge in opening the case.

IN THE WEST WIGAN COUNTY COURT                    CASE NO. 1630817

BETWEEN:

MARY ACTON                    Claimant

and

JEREMY BENTHAM                    Defendant

PARTICULARS OF CLAIM

1.   The Claimant is the owner of the freehold property known as Jade Fields, Water Lane, West Wigan, Surrey (below called 'Jade Fields') shown coloured pink on the plan annexed hereto. The Defendant is the owner-occupier of the property known as Amber Acre, Pearl Lane, West Wigan, Surrey (below called 'Amber Acre') shown coloured blue on the plan annexed hereto.

2.   If contrary to the Claimant's contentions below she is not the legal owner of the whole of Jade Fields she has been in occupation of the whole of the property which she now occupies since on or about January 1961 and she has now acquired possessory title to that part of Jade Fields which she does not have the legal title to. The Claimant will rely on evidence that her family had from about 1960 until 1979 without any objections from the Defendant or the Defendant's successor in title treated the ditch area as her own. The acts relied upon include: walking along the ditch to visit occupiers of Topaz Cottage; trimming and caring for the ditch; planting flowers along the side of the ditch; visitors playing in the ditch, collecting leaves and leaving bicycles there.

3.   Any use of the ditch area by the Defendant or the Defendant's successor in title such as occasionally trimming the hedge on the north boundary, using the ditch to drain water when another drain was flooded and allowing children to play there were minimal interferences with the Claimant's occupation and were all carried out after permission of the Claimant had been sought and granted.

4.   The Claimant has erected a fence along the northern boundary of Jade Fields adjoining Amber Acre in the approximate position marked A/B on the plan.

5.   The Defendant has trespassed on Jade Fields by entering on to the Claimant's property situated to the south of the line A/B against the Claimant's wishes and damaging the Claimant's property.

PARTICULARS OF DAMAGE

(a)   Damage to and destruction of parts of the Claimant's fence.
(b)   Damage to and destruction of flowers growing near the Claimant's fence.
(c)   Build-up of rubbish and debris and partial blocking of the drain situated in Jade Fields.

AND THE CLAIMANT CLAIMS:

(i)     Damages limited to £5,000.
(ii)    Interest pursuant to section 69 of the County Courts Act 1984 at the rate of 15% per annum.
(iii)   An injunction restraining the Defendant from entering upon any part of the Claimant's property known as Jade Fields.
(iv)   A declaration that the Claimant is the legal and beneficial owner of Jade Fields.
(v)    Further and other relief.
(vi)   Costs.

STATEMENT OF TRUTH

The claimant believes that the facts stated in this application are true

Signed        P Stockington           Partner
                     Claimant's solicitor       Stockingtons
                                               82 High Street
                                               West Wigan
                                               Surrey

Dated 1 August 1999

To the court and the defendant

IN THE WEST WIGAN COUNTY COURT          CASE NO. 1630817

BETWEEN:

MARY ACTON                                                    Claimant

and

JEREMY BENTHAM                                          Defendant

### DEFENCE

1.   Save that it is not admitted that the boundaries of Amber Acre are accurately shown coloured blue on the plan annexed to the Particulars of Claim paragraph 1 of the Particulars of Claim is admitted.

2.   Paragraph 2 of the Particulars of Claim is denied. For the reasons set out in the counterclaim below the Defendant claims that he is the legal and beneficial owner of the hedge and ditch area. It is contended that trimming and caring for the ditch was undertaken by the Claimant, her late husband, and the Defendant's predecessor in title, Mrs Diamond once or twice a year and who carried out the work varied as a result of a consensual neighbourly agreement which had no effect and was not intended by any party to have an effect on the legal or beneficial ownership of the land.

3.   The Defendant concurs that all the acts referred to in paragraph 3 took place but denies that permission was sought and given on each occasion or that the acts constituted minimal interference. In particular it is contended that the Defendant never asked for permission for the children to play and evidence will be given by Jane Diamond the daughter of the Defendant's predecessor in title that the area was used for drainage on many occasions without permission.

4.   Save that it is admitted that the Claimant has erected a fence paragraph 4 of the Particulars of Claim is not admitted. The fence was erected by the Claimant in 1997 without the Defendant's permission on the northern side of a ditch belonging to the Defendant and several feet to the north of an established boundary hedge belonging to the Claimant which ran along the northern boundary of the Claimant's property Jade Fields in the approximate position marked A/B on the plan annexed to the Particulars of Claim.

5.   Paragraph 5 of the Particulars of Claim is denied. The freehold title to the land referred to is and was at all material times vested in the Defendant.

6.   Further or alternatively if the freehold title to all or any part of the land referred to was not vested in the Defendant and his predecessor in title to Amber Acre he has acquired possessory title through uninterrupted possession for over 20 years.

### COUNTERCLAIM

1.   The Defendant claims to be the owner of the hedge and ditch referred to in the Particulars of Claim and clearly indicated in the plan annexed to the deed of conveyance of Amber Lodge dated 6th July 1910 and made between Ruby Entwhistle (1) and Mabel Keith (2). A copy of the 1910 plan is annexed to this counterclaim.

2.   The Defendant and his predecessors in title have consistently maintained that he she or they were and are the lawful owners of the hedge and ditch.

3.   The Claimant has recently trespassed on the Defendant's land and wrongfully erected a fence contrary to the express wishes of the Defendant.

AND THE DEFENDANT COUNTERCLAIMS:

(a)   Damages limited to £5,000.

(b)   Interest pursuant to section 69 of the County Courts Act 1984 at 15% per annum.

(c)   An injunction restraining the Claimant from entering any part of the Defendant's property Amber Acre.

(d)   A declaration that the Defendant is the legal and beneficial owner of the ditch which separates Amber Acre from Jade Fields.

(e)   Further or other relief.

(f)   Costs.

STATEMENT OF TRUTH

The defendant believes that the facts stated in this defence are true

Signed          Z.A. Brown                            Partner
                Defendant's solicitor                 Morecrofts
                                                       87 High Street
                                                       West Wigan
                                                       Surrey

Dated 18th August 1999

IN THE WEST WIGAN COUNTY COURT                    CASE NO. 1630817

BETWEEN:

MARY ACTON                                      Claimant

and

JEREMY BENTHAM                                  Defendant

REPLY

Save and in so far as the Defence contains admissions, the Claimant joins issue with every statement made in the Defence.

DEFENCE TO THE COUNTERCLAIM

1.  Paragraph 1 of the Counterclaim is not admitted.

2.  Paragraphs 2 and 3 of the Counterclaim are denied. The Claimant has erected a fence but contends the land is owned by him and so he is entitled to do this.

Stockingtons
82 High Street
West Wigan
Surrey

Dated this 26th day of August 1999

REPORT ON THE BOUNDARIES

at

Jade Fields, Water Lane, West Wigan, Surrey

Minters
Chartered Surveyors
West Wigan
Surrey

INTRODUCTION
I have been instructed in this matter by solicitors to Mrs Acton to advise on the correct position of the northern boundary of the property owned by Mrs Acton.

DOCUMENTS AND PLANS
I have been provided with a copy of the Land Registry Plan with a filed title number WW 33621. A photocopy of that plan is attached hereto on which I have shown outlined in red, the property owned by Mrs Acton and in blue, that understood to be owned by Mr Bentham. I have been provided with other documents and plans relating to the ownership of the property owned by Mr Bentham and copies of these plans are attached hereto also. I have also been provided with a copy of the title relating to a property known as Topaz Cottage in Water Lane, again a copy of the plan annexed to that is attached. For purposes of identification, these plans are identified as follows:

1. Land Registry Plan — LA 1.
2. Plan of part of Mr Bentham's property — LA 2.
3. Plan of remaining part of Mr Bentham's property — LA 3.
4. Plan of Topaz Cottage — LA 4.

SITE INSPECTION
I have made two inspections of the site, on one occasion in the company of the surveyor to Mr Bentham. Measurements have been taken to verify the dimensions shown on the Land Registry Plan LA 1, and in an attempt to check the eastern boundary, the total dimension distances from Water Lane of 51ft. and 49ft. were taken in an attempt to position the north eastern corner.

Attached to this report is a sketch that I have prepared showing the dimensions taken on site when I visited and these tie up to the dimensions shown on the Land Registry Plan.

Some slight doubt over the exact position of the southern boundary can exist. The angle irons at corners of the fence are set approximately 6″ from driven galvanised piping and which I believe more accurately reflects the boundary position and being probably the original piping driven to mark the corners of the plot when it was sub-divided. If this is the case, the northern boundary would be again approximately 5″ to 6″ further to the north than that which was originally thought.

PHOTOGRAPHS
I attach hereto a series of photographs taken on site and also a sketch plan showing the approximate location from which each photograph was taken. These photographs clearly show the galvanised pipes to which I make earlier reference. Also shown, is the overgrown nature of the boundary between the two properties.

CONCLUSION
From measurements that I have taken on site, I conclude that the position of the boundary in accordance with the Land Registry Title Plan is approximately 4ft. to the north of the hedge, approximately 19ft. from the north east corner of the dwelling known as 'Jade Fields' and running in a straight line to the south east corner of the single storey addition on the property known as 'Topaz Cottage'.

I have also to conclude that the position of the north east boundary would tie in with that, having taken measurements of approximately 100ft. from the Water Lane frontage, having allowed approximately 2′ 6″ for the 'set back' to the top of the retaining wall. In checking that measurement, the lack of any firm reference point at the Water Lane frontage does make for some measurement difficulty.

Since my initial inspection and measurements were taken, the line of the boundary under dispute has become overgrown and is being used as a refuse and garden tip, seemingly in an attempt to gain ownership. This area will need to be cleared before the boundary can be clearly pegged and fenced.

Signed:. . . . . . . . . . .
L. Allen FRICS
Minters
3 High Street
West Wigan
Surrey

Dated: 1 August 1999

BOUNDARY BETWEEN
Jade Fields, Water Lane and Amber Acre, Pearl Lane,
West Wigan, Surrey

EXPLANATORY NOTES to plan showing the boundary as measured and staked with 3 stakes by L. Allen FRICS and S. Shaw FRICS.

## GENERAL
The boundary to be from the boundary with the property to the east, through the three stakes inserted, to the west end being 4″ west of the third (western most) stake.

## STAKE 1 .
In view of the difficulty of measurement a series of measurements were taken from the base of the wall in Water Lane, not edge of kerb, to a fence on top of the wall, to a shed, both not permanent, near to and parallel with the east boundary, this line being about 2′ 3″ from the east boundary when in line with the south wall of the extension to Jade Fields, continued to 100′ where a stake inserted near the south side of the ditch. Measurement taken to a galvanised post on the south boundary of Amber Acre, 46′ 9″ and not 49′ 0″ as shown on Land Certificate. Measurement taken from the stake to south west corner of Jade Fields, 49′.

## STAKE 2
Stake inserted to south edge of ditch line with east wall of Amber Acre. Measurements taken from stake to south west corner of Jade Fields, 36′ 6″, south east corner of extension of Mercott, 44′ 11″ and north east corner of Amber Acre, 15′ 3″, the difference of this measurement from the previous joint measurement gives widths of Amber Acre of 52′ 5″ and 73′ 5″ as shown on plan and not as detailed on Land Certificate.

## STAKE 3
Stake inserted in line with apparent south edge of ditch 4″ east of line with east wall of lean-to extension of Topaz Cottage, this point being the true west end of the south boundary of Jade Fields, situated in the substantial growth of the offset section of hedge. Measurements taken from the stake to the south west corner of Topaz Cottage, 27′ 2″, south east corner of Topaz Cottage, 3′ 5″ and south west corner of Jade Fields, 124′ 8″.

Further check and survey measurements in files of both surveyors.

L Allen FRICS                                                                                          S Shaw FRICS

1 August 1999

# H.M. LAND REGISTRY

Scale 1/1250.  Enlarged from 1/2500.

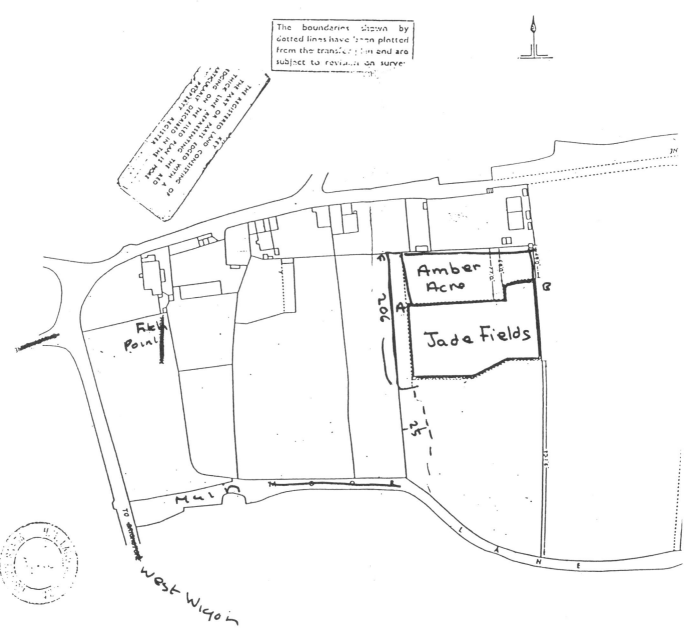

Parish West Wigan
OS Sheet Sussex (Wigan) XCVI 3
Crown Copyright Reserved
Filed Plan of Title No. WW33621

# FOUR

# MORTGAGES

## 4.1 Introduction

The law on mortgages is full of complex little backwaters of much academic interest. Fortunately for most barristers they are unlikely to have to deal with the more abstruse points, particularly in their early years of practice. Nevertheless mortgage repossessions are part of the staple diet of many a young Chancery practitioner and claims by a co-owner or occupier that he should not be bound by a mortgage agreement are currently rather popular. It is also often important in reviewing possible professional negligence in conveyancing transactions to have a good knowledge of how a mortgage should work.

## 4.2 Creation of a Mortgage

### 4.2.1 LAW OF PROPERTY ACT 1925, S. 87: CHARGE BY WAY OF LEGAL MORTGAGE

This is by far the most important, and most frequently used, method of creating a mortgage in practice. This procedure of creating a mortgage operates both for freehold and leasehold land. It provides the same 'protection, powers and remedies' (s. 87(2)) as a mortgage made under ss. 85 or 86. The 1925 Act contains an example of the document, which, when executed, will create a charge by way of legal mortgage (sch. 5, Form 1). Most institutional lenders will adopt a document with many more terms. Typically, it is standard for there to be a list of covenants between mortgagor and mortgagee. A number of these (not to grant leases, take in paying guests, etc.) are designed to minimise the risks to the lender of some person obtaining an overriding interest by virtue of an equitable interest coupled with occupation (see LRA 1925, s. 70(1)(g)). To protect themselves, lenders will make standard inquiries of the persons who occupy the mortgaged premises with the mortgagor to disclose any equitable interests that such third parties may have (most often this will be with cohabitees, partners, children etc.). The mortgage document will also contain detailed provisions as to the repayment of capital and interest, usually by instalments over the prescribed period. In addition, it is common for there to be a requirement that the mortgagor take out life insurance (at his own expense) which will be sufficient, in the event of his death, to repay the outstanding capital and interest.

### 4.2.2 LAW OF PROPERTY ACT 1925, SS. 85 AND 86

It is also possible to create a legal mortgage by creation of a long lease in freehold land, or a sublease in leasehold land (LPA 1925, ss. 85, 86).

### 4.2.3 EQUITABLE MORTGAGES

#### 4.2.3.1 Contract to create a mortgage
Following the maxim that 'Equity will regard as done that which ought to be done', an equitable mortgage can arise where the mortgagor enters into a specifically enforceable agreement to create a legal mortgage. However, there are procedural requirements

which should be observed. Transactions entered into before 27 September 1989 must be shown to comply with the LPA 1925, s. 40 (evidenced in writing and/or by part performance in pursuance). If made after 26 September 1989, the transaction must comply with the Law of Property (Miscellaneous Provisions) Act (LP(MP)A) 1989, s. 2, and be in writing and signed by *both* parties. (A document is not signed by a company merely by being on the company's headed paper: *Firstpost Homes Ltd* v *Johnson* [1995] 4 All ER 355, CA.)

### 4.2.3.2 Deposit of the title deeds

It had been accepted since *Russell* v *Russell* (1783) 1 Bro CC 269 that an equitable mortgage could be created by delivery of the title deeds of the security to the lender, provided it could be shown that the mortgagor intended the property to be security. Prior to the enactment of the LP(MP)A 1989, s. 2, the deposit of the deeds was a sufficient act of part performance under the LPA 1925, s. 40, to avoid the need for a memorandum. Section 2(1) of the 1989 Act now prescribes that 'a contract for the sale or other disposition of land can only be made in writing' and s. 2(3) requires that it be signed by both parties. It is no longer sufficient to satisfy s. 2 to have the oral contract reduced to writing at some later date, or simply to deposit the title deeds.

Some textbook writers have questioned whether creation by deposit of title deeds is governed by s. 2. However, recent first-instance authority has confirmed the view that mortgages can no longer be created by depositing the title deeds. In *United Bank of Kuwait plc* v *Sahib* [1997] Ch 107 Chadwick J held that there was no authority to support the argument that a security would be created by the deposit of the title deeds rather than by agreement. The effect of the LP(MP)A 1989, s. 2, was that there could be no creation of an equitable charge which was not contract based. Further, even if an equitable charge could be created by a deposit of the title deeds, the LPA 1925, s. 53(1)(c), would operate to make void any disposition not in writing. This decision was confirmed by the Court of Appeal. In light of this decision, practitioners should ensure that a deposit of the title deeds is accompanied by a memorandum in writing which complies with s. 2 of the 1989 Act. If a mortgage is held to be ineffective for want of the requirements in s. 2, subject to the terms of the loan, the effect may be that the loan becomes immediately repayable.

### 4.2.3.3 Mortgage of an equitable interest

After the 1925 legislation, certain interests in land were equitable only (e.g., the beneficial interest under a trust for sale or strict settlement). However, such interests have a value, can be sold, and can therefore provide adequate security for a mortgage. The procedure for creating mortgages of equitable interests was not affected by the 1925 legislation, and so such mortgages continue to be created by the transfer of the entire interest to the mortgagee with a covenant that such interest be returned upon repayment of the loan. However, the LPA 1925, s. 53(1)(c), does require that such a transfer be in writing, signed by the mortgagor, to be valid.

# 4.3 Rights of the Mortgagor

## 4.3.1 RIGHT TO REDEEM

At law, the redemption date may be provided in the mortgage agreement. The mortgagor has the right to repay the amount of the loan on this date, but only on this date. Under equity, the mortgagor was permitted to redeem the mortgage after the date fixed by the agreement. Modern mortgages often contain a timetable for repayments by instalments. Such terms will allow for the amounts of repayments to vary to accommodate factors such as the rise and fall of interest rates, or graduated repayments, but most agreements will provide that if there is a default on an instalment, then the mortgagee can insist on repayment of the whole sum outstanding.

The mortgagor retains the legal title to the property, but subject to the rights of the mortgagee. The mortgagor owns the 'equity of redemption'. This should not be confused with the equitable right to redeem, which is one of the rights comprised in the mortgaged land. The right to occupation will usually be conferred on the mortgagor by a term in the mortgage.

### 4.3.2   RESTRICTIONS ON REDEMPTION

The courts have developed a number of rules which have as their root the principle that the mortgagee is entitled to take the security only to secure repayment of the mortgage. Any term which seeks to prevent the mortgagor from redeeming will be void. Similarly, terms which purport to delay the mortgagor's right to redeem are viewed with suspicion and may be cut down. As a mortgagor has no right in equity to redeem before the legal date of redemption (save certain short-term, low-value mortgages which are caught by the Consumer Credit Act 1974, which can be redeemed at any time), there have been examples where mortgagees have set a very late date for the contractual date of redemption. Much will depend on the relationship of the mortgagee and mortgagor. In *Knightsbridge Estates Trust Ltd* v *Byrne* [1939] Ch 441 the Court of Appeal, in allowing a postponement of the legal date by 40 years between an institutional lender and a business, held that the test was not whether the postponement was reasonable, but whether the contract had been entered freely, in an arm's length transaction. In the domestic mortgage market there is likely to be an enormous disparity between the bargaining power of the mortgagor and mortgagee, which would invite the court's intervention. In practice, however, it is unlikely that an institutional lender dealing in the domestic market would attempt to impose such a clause.

### 4.3.3   COLLATERAL ADVANTAGES FOR THE MORTGAGEE

If there are contractual terms imposed on the mortgagor, these must not be oppressive or unconscionable, and may only last for the duration of the mortgage. Different standards will apply to the commercial mortgage sector from the domestic market. Provided they do not offend the domestic or European rules on anti-competitive business practices, ties in a mortgage of a public house which oblige the mortgagor to obtain his supplies from the brewery (mortgagee) are legitimate, and the restrictions this imposes on the mortgagor, providing there is not a wide disparity in bargaining power, are likely to have been taken into account in negotiations and reflected in the interest rate and/or the term granted to the mortgagor. The agreement must be unfair and unconscionable, not merely unreasonable, before the court will interfere: *Multiservice Bookbinding Ltd* v *Marden* [1979] Ch 84. In the domestic market, individuals have statutory protection under ss. 137 to 140 of the Consumer Credit Act 1974, which empower the court to reopen any credit agreement (including a mortgage) which it finds to be extortionate, and to 'do justice between the parties'.

### 4.3.4   POWER TO GRANT LEASES

The statutory power is contained in the LPA 1925, s. 99, and is subject to the conditions set out there. In the domestic market, institutional lenders will usually prohibit the mortgagor from granting leases so that complications cannot be created by the presence of a sitting tenant. It is, however, reasonably common for lenders to permit their mortgagors to lease the property on short-term contracts (usually assured shorthold under the Housing Act 1988) as this can have the advantage for the lender of a steady income to the mortgagor to support the mortgage repayments, together with the speedy possession procedure should the mortgagee need to sell with vacant possession. Different considerations may apply to commercial premises, particularly if the mortgagor intends to lease the mortgaged property as part of its commercial activity.

## 4.4   Rights of the Mortgagee

### 4.4.1   TO HOLD THE TITLE DEEDS

Modern mortgages do not require the mortgagor to transfer his interest in the property to the mortgagee. Consequently, the mortgagee would not, as a matter of course, obtain the deeds to the security. However, under the LPA 1925, ss. 85 to 87, the first mortgagee can require delivery of the title deeds. In practice, institutional lenders will insist on this being done. In registered land, the mortgagee must protect its interests by registration of the mortgage against the title, and will obtain a charge certificate: LRA 1925, s. 65. Any subsequent mortgages purportedly created will take subject to charges on the register.

### 4.4.2 TO POSSESSION OF THE PROPERTY

As mortgages are created by the granting of a lease or sublease (or are to be treated as having been so granted), prima facie the mortgagee (as a lessee) has the right to occupy the premises from the moment when the mortgage is executed: LPA 1925, s. 95(4). As explained by Harman J in *Four-Maids Ltd* v *Dudley Marshall (Properties) Ltd* [1957] Ch 317:

> The right of a mortgagee to possession in the absence of some contract has nothing to do with default on the part of the mortgagor. The mortgagee may go into possession before the ink is dry on the mortgage unless there is something in the contract, express or implied, whereby he has contracted himself out of that right. He has the right because he has a legal term of years in the property.

However, as the whole purpose of domestic mortgages is to provide a home for the mortgagor, the right to possession is usually suspended on condition that the mortgagor keeps up the mortgage repayments. If the term suspending the right of possession is broken (e.g., by failure to keep up repayments) then the mortgagee can *peaceably* take possession. Usually, this necessitates an order from the court (as the mortgagee is not permitted to enter a dwellinghouse by force), and the court will consider all the factors (see **4.5.8** *et seq.*). However, if the mortgagee can obtain possession peaceably, the mortgagor cannot claim the protection of the Administration of Justice Act 1970, s. 36: *Ropaigealach* v *Barclays Bank plc* [1999] 3 WLR 17.

### 4.4.3 TO LEASE

The power to lease only arises where the mortgagee has taken possession (see **4.6.2**).

### 4.4.4 TO REQUIRE THAT THE PROPERTY BE INSURED

This requirement is likely to be written into standard mortgage agreements, and is designed to protect the value of the security from loss in value due to damage. The mortgagor will bear the cost of the insurance policy. In the absence of a formal term, LPA 1925, s. 101(1)(ii), implies a term into every mortgage agreement permitting the mortgagee to obtain insurance, the premium on which can be added to the amount to be repaid on the mortgage.

### 4.4.5 TO TACK AND CONSOLIDATE

## 4.5 Remedies of the Mortgagee

### 4.5.1 GENERALLY

When the mortgagor has defaulted on a term in the mortgage agreement (usually to keep to the timetable of repayments), the mortgagee may pursue any or all of the following remedies. However, it should be remembered that there will always be scope for negotiation with institutional lenders, provided the mortgagor can show a willingness and ability to make up the arrears. Possession actions are expensive for lenders, not only in terms of legal costs but also in the losses that will be sustained by a forced sale of the security, particularly when property markets are depressed.

Care must be taken in choosing between High Court and county court proceedings. In claims for possession the county court has exclusive jurisdiction in relation to dwelling houses outside Greater London. The High Court and the county court have concurrent jurisdiction in claims for possession of dwelling houses within Greater London and other types of property wherever situate. In claims for payment the High Court and the county court have concurrent jurisdiction. In claims for foreclosure, redemption or sale the county court jurisdiction is limited (unless extended by agreement) to cases where the amount owing is under £30,000.

All mortgage actions now have to be commenced by a claim form. They can be in either CPR, Part 7 or Part 8 form. It is likely that the vast majority will be commenced using Part 8 form (as previously most were commenced using an originating summons). Where there is likely to be substantial issues of fact such as claims that the charge should be set aside because of undue influence, then Part 8 proceedings will be more appropriate. Mortgage proceedings are governed by the re-enacted RSC O. 88.

## 4.5.2 DEMAND PAYMENT OF PRINCIPAL AND INTEREST

As a mortgage is a contract between the mortgagor and mortgagee, the mortgagee can sue in contract for payment of the whole sum outstanding following a default. This is only likely to be relevant in a handful of commercial cases where a company mortgagor has sufficient assets to pay off the outstanding mortgage. In most other cases the mortgagor does not have the assets to clear the outstanding mortgage; usually the reason he has taken out a mortgage in the first place.

In most cases where the lender is granted possession the lender will also get a money judgment. If possession is suspended on terms, the money judgment will usually be suspended on the same terms: *Cheltenham and Gloucester Building Society* v *Grattidge* (1993) 25 HLR 454. But if possession is suspended on the ground that the borrower has a reasonable prospect of being able to repay the full amount shortly by selling the property, the application for a money judgment may be adjourned: *National and Provincial Building Society* v *Lloyd* [1996] 1 All ER 630.

## 4.5.3 FORECLOSURE

Foreclosure actions are far less common in practice than possession actions. The remedy is only available where the contractual date for redemption has passed and there has been a breach of the obligation to repay. The effect of an order for foreclosure is to vest the title to the property in the mortgagee and to extinguish the liability of the mortgagor on the loan. Where, as in the vast majority of cases, the outstanding mortgage is a fraction of the value of the property that would vest, LPA 1925, s. 91(2) allows the mortgagor to ask the court to grant an order for sale instead of foreclosure. The balance of the proceeds of sale following the discharge of the mortgage, plus costs, is repaid to the mortgagor by the lender. Given that the standard practice of the court is to accede to requests for an order for sale, the modern practice, to save costs, is for the mortgagee to seek an order for possession and sale in one application.

## 4.5.4 APPOINTMENT OF A RECEIVER

Section 109(1) of the LPA 1925 empowers the mortgagee to appoint a receiver to collect the income from the managed property. This right arises after the contractual date for redemption, and can be exercised whether the mortgagee is in possession or not. Importantly, the receiver is deemed by statute to be the agent of the *mortgagor* (s. 109(2)), and so the mortgagee, although responsible for the appointment, is not responsible for what the receiver does in the management of the property, unless the mortgagee interferes with the activities of the receiver: *American Express International Banking Corporation* v *Hurley* [1985] 3 All ER 564. The appointment of a receiver can therefore relieve the mortgagee of the duties he would otherwise have to observe in possession of the property (see **4.6.3**). However, the mortagor may have a claim against the receiver: *Medforth* v *Blake* [1999] 3 All ER 97, CA (see **4.5.8.2**).

## 4.5.5 POWER OF SALE

The power for the mortgagee to sell the security is implied into every agreement by the LPA 1925, s. 101(1)(i), and arises:

(a) when the mortgage has been made by deed; and

(b) the legal date of redemption has passed (where the mortgage is by instalment this will be when a payment is overdue); and

(c) there is no contrary intention expressed in the mortgage.

### 4.5.6 EXERCISE OF POWER OF SALE

Once the power of sale has arisen, it can be exercised when one of these conditions is satisfied (s. 103):

(a) default on capital instalment for three months after the notice has been served; or

(b) some of the interest payable is at least two months in arrears; or

(c) breach of a covenant in the mortgage deed (other than to keep up with the repayments).

### 4.5.7 PROCEDURE FOR SALE

The statutory power of sale may be exercised without a court order. However, institutional lenders will rarely wish to exercise the right of sale alone. To maximise the value of the security, the lender will wish to sell the property with vacant possession. As an order for possession can only be granted by the court, it is standard practice for the mortgagee to apply for an order for possession and sale (under s. 91) in one application.

The mortgagee owes a duty of care to the mortgagor in the exercise of the power of sale. The duty is owed in equity and not in negligence (*Parker-Tweedale* v *Dunbar Bank plc (No. 1)* [1991] Ch 12), and it appears it can be excluded by a clause in the mortgage agreement (*Bishop* v *Bonham* [1988] 1 WLR 742). In *Cuckmere Brick Co. Ltd* v *Mutual Finance Ltd* [1971] Ch 949 the Court of Appeal held that a mortgagee would be liable to the mortgagor for a failure to obtain a 'market' price for the property. However, the court recognised that it was for the mortgagee to decide the time to sell, and so the mortgagee could not be liable for choosing a 'bad' time in the year. However, in *Standard Chartered Bank Ltd* v *Walker* [1982] 1 WLR 1410 the Court of Appeal decided that mortgagees could be liable for any negligence in the handling of the sale, including (per Lord Denning) negligence in choosing a poor time to sell. Section 13(7) of the Building Societies Act 1986 imposes an obligation on building society mortgagees to secur 'the best price that can reasonably be obtained', but they are not required to wait for a more favourable time of year: *Reliance Permanent Building Society* v *Harwood-Stamper* [1944] Ch 362.

On sale, the mortgagee conveys the charged estate free of the mortgage, any interests of the mortgagor and any other interests over which the mortgage has priority.

### 4.5.8 POSSESSION

#### 4.5.8.1 Procedure

This remedy is available both for legal and equitable mortgages. Second (and subsequent) mortgagees can take possession subject to the rights of the superior mortgagees. Where a mortgagee seeks possession in order to sell under either a term in the agreement or pursuant to the statutory power, this is the only relief that needs to be claimed. The newly re-enacted RSC O. 88 details the evidence required and imposes time limits on the various stages.

#### 4.5.8.2 Principles governing possession actions

Institutional lenders will only usually commence possession proceedings where the relationship with the customer has broken down and there is serious or repeated default without the prospect of the arrears being paid off. The effect of a successful application for possession in the domestic market is that the mortgagor (and usually his family) lose their home. The court will always proceed carefully on hearing such applications, and quite properly demand from those representing the mortgagee that all the procedural requirements have been followed. Other methods of recouping arrears should generally be tried first: *Cheltenham and Gloucester Building Society* v *Norgan* [1996] 1 WLR 343, CA. Otherwise the mortgagor may find itself penalised in relation to the costs of the possession hearing: *Abbey National plc* v *Acharya* [1996] CLY 4979.

Upon the application for possession of a dwelling house the Administration of Justice Act 1970, s. 36 empowers the court to adjourn the proceedings or stay execution of the order for possession if it appears that the mortgagor is likely to be able within a reasonable period to pay any sums due under the mortgage. The 'sums due' are the instalments in arrears, and the court can ignore a clause which deems the whole sum to be due upon a single default: Administration of Justice Act 1973, s. 8.

Essentially the court will be looking for evidence that the mortgagee's security is adequately protected and that it is likely to be receiving all the money due at some reasonable time or some money due soon with the expectation of instalments being resumed and arrears paid off.

In deciding what is a reasonable time the court will look at the amount of arrears, the length of the mortgage term and the amount of equity in the property. It is important in acting for either side to get a realistic valuation of the property. In *Cheltenham and Gloucester Building Society* v *Norgan* the court considered that there was no particular limit to what could constitute a reasonable period and in an appropriate case it could mean the whole of the remaining term of the mortgage. Although judges, particularly since *Norgan*, may have taken a more lenient view of the length of time which can be considered reasonable, good evidence is required. See also *Skandia Financial Services* v *Greenfield* [1997] CLY 4248.

It is possible for a court to suspend possession under s. 36 on the ground that the property will be sold in a reasonable time and that there is a reasonable prospect that the proceeds will be sufficent to pay off the sums due: *Bristol and West Building Society* v *Ellis* (1996) 73 P & CR 158; *Target Home Loans Ltd* v *Clothier* [1994] 1 All ER 439. If the proceeds are unlikely to pay off the whole sum then possession cannot be suspended but the mortgagee could still apply to have conduct of the sale of the property under the LPA 1925, s. 91.

Even if possession is suspended by virtue of the Administration of Justice Act 1970, s. 36, conduct of the sale may still be given to the mortgagor in an application under the LPA 1925, s. 91.

In a potentially far-reaching decision the Court of Appeal decided that the protection of s. 36 only applies where a mortgagee has sought an order for possession, not where they had exercised their common law right to take possession peaceably: *Ropaigealach* v *Barclays Bank plc* [1999] 3 WLR 17. Less scrupulous lenders may find this a useful way of circumventing the protection offered to residential mortgagors.

## 4.6  The Mortgagee in Possession

### 4.6.1  SELLING THE PROPERTY

As seen above, the standard practice is for banks and building societies to seek orders for possession and sale in one application. There is quite likely, however, to be a period when the mortgagee gains possession and is waiting for a buyer, and during that period the mortgagor is responsible for the proper management of the property.

### 4.6.2  LEASING THE PROPERTY

Institutional lenders usually take possession only to realise the security (i.e. to sell it). Banks and building societies rarely wish to become landlords/managers of a proliferation of properties. However, in recent years because of the very unfavourable property market, it has made commercial sense to take possession from mortgagors in arrears, and then lease the properties out on short-term contracts; particularly in London where there is a large and fairly fluid lettings market. This is also attractive to lenders because of the difference between possession and foreclosure. Although in the mortgagor's eyes they both amount to losing his house, where the mortgagor merely takes possession and leases out the property, the mortgagor is still liable to make repayments and pay interest. The potential for hardship to the mortgagor in such circumstances has been recognised by the Court of Appeal. In *Palk* v *Mortgage Service Funding plc* [1993] Ch 330, it was held that where it was in the best interests of the mortgagor that the property be sold, such would be ordered by the court, even if the property market were depressed and the mortgagee was opposed to the sale. In the domestic market, unless the mortgagee and mortgagor come to some arrangement whereby their relationship is converted (perhaps in the short term) to that of lessor and lessee, possession by the lender followed by letting will never be in the best interests of the mortgagor.

### 4.6.3 DUTIES OF THE MORTGAGEE IN POSSESSION

The mortgagee is required to manage the property properly. The mortgagee may use the income arising from the land to pay off the interest and capital and will be liable for any mismanagement of the property or waste. The test is whether the mortgagee has been guilty of wilful default. The mortgagee is under a duty to account strictly to the mortgagor for the period of possession. If a mortgagee intends to take possession for a lengthy period (usually only in commercial premises) it may be more appropriate to appoint a receiver (see **4.5.4**). A mortgagee in possession who lets the property at an undervalue may be held liable for the difference between the rent charged and a proper market rent.

## 4.7 Problems with Equitable Mortgages

It should be noted that where a mortgage is equitable there may be problems with the methods of enforcement, though these are eased if the mortgage is supported by a deed (as then the LPA 1925, s. 101 will apply). The main problems are whether there is a right to possession and whether the equitable mortgagee can convey the legal estate to a purchaser: *Barclays Bank Ltd* v *Bird* [1954] Ch 274, 280; *Ex parte Bignold* (1834) 4 Deac & Ch 259; *Re White Rose Cottage* [1965] Ch 940. Most problems can be overcome by making an application to the court for the necessary power, but this can prove expensive, and most of the cost falls to be met by the mortgagor.

## 4.8 Priorities in Relation to Mortgages

In the case of a mortgage of an equitable interest, priority depends upon the date at which notice is given to the trustees: *Dearle* v *Hall* (1823) 3 Russ 1.

For mortgages of the legal estate, the priority order between mortgages, or between a mortgage and other interest, basically depends upon the usual rules for priority in registered/unregistered land. However, the natural order of priority can be avoided where there is evidence of fraud (*Peter* v *Russel* (1716) 1 Eq Cas Abr 321) or negligence (*Walker* v *Linom* [1907] 2 Ch 10) on the part of the mortgagee. It should be remembered that the cases and priorities are difficult to reconcile and will require careful investigation in dealing with any problem.

## 4.9 Undue Influence in Mortgage Transactions

The doctrine of undue influence provides a fruitful area for dispute in mortgage transactions. A considerable amount of litigation was (and is still being) generated as a result of the property slump of the late 1980s and early 1990s. There is no relevant statutory authority in this area. In researching a problem in this area it is essential to start with the principles as explained in the two guideline cases of *Barclays Bank plc v O'Brien* [1994] 1 AC 180 and *CIBC Mortgages plc v Pitt* [1994] 1 AC 200. Cases decided prior to these should be used with great caution although they may be helpful on particular points. There is a steady stream of reported cases in this area which apply and/or explain the application of the principles outlined in *Pitt* and *O'Brien* to a variety of fact situations. It is especially important in this area to ensure that you have checked for the very latest authorities.

## 4.9.1    RELATIONSHIP BETWEEN THE PARTIES

It is necessary to consider first what is the nature of the relationship between the alleged victim of undue influence and the other property owner. Does it fall within the recognised categories where undue influence is automatically presumed? If not, is it a relationship which is capable of being one of 'trust and confidence' and so giving rise to a presumption of undue influence (many of the reported cases deal with relationships in this category — usually spouses, and child and elderly parent). Further if it is capable of being a relationship of 'trust and confidence' is there evidence that this in fact existed.

If no presumption of undue influence can be established then it is necessary to consider actual undue influence (below).

## 4.9.2    ADDITIONAL REQUIREMENTS FOR CASES OF PRESUMED UNDUE INFLUENCE

If presumed undue influence exists then it is for the borrower to show that the transaction was manifestly to his disadvantage. To rebut the presumption, the other property owner (or the lender) has to show that the transaction was entered into as a result of the 'free exercise of an independent will': *Inche Noriah v Shaikh Allie Bin Omar* [1929] AC 127. This usually turns upon whether the borrower was given a realistic opportunity to obtain independent legal advice.

## 4.9.3    ACTUAL UNDUE INFLUENCE

In order to establish actual undue influence, the victim must prove:

(a)   the exertion of undue influence; and

(b)   that the borrower would not have entered into the transaction but for the exercise of the undue influence: *Bank of Credit and Commerce International SA v Aboody* [1990] 1 QB 923.

There is no requirement that manifest disadvantage be shown.

## 4.9.4    NOTICE OF UNDUE INFLUENCE

Most disputes arise between a lender and borrower. The undue influence has usually been exerted by a cohabitee or close family member. To defend an action by the lender on the grounds of undue influence, the borrower must show that the undue influence was exerted by the lender, or the lender's agents, or the lender had notice that the undue influence was being exerted.

A crucial issue in respect of both types of undue influence is, therefore, the circumstances in which a lender can be fixed with notice of undue influence by others. As regards cohabitees (both married and unmarried) the steps which it is sufficient for a lender to take are set out in *Barclays Bank plc v O'Brien*. A lender can avoid being fixed with notice of undue influence if it has advised the cohabitee on *both* the following points:

(a)   of the nature of the transaction and its consequences;

(b)   to seek independent legal advice as to the transaction.

A lender will generally be entitled to rely on the fact that a person has received legal advice and will not be imputed with any constructive notice of undue influence the legal advice is alleged to have had. However, this does not apply where the legal adviser is acting as agent for the lender and so if the lender has instructed a legal adviser acting for itself and the other property owner to tell the alleged victim to take independent advice and the legal adviser has neglected to do this adequately or at all, the legal adviser is likely to be considered to be an agent for the lender and any constructive notice of undue influence can be imputed to the lender. See *Royal Bank of Scotland plc* v *Etridge (No. 2)* (1998) *The Times*, 17 August 1998.

## 4.9.5   REMEDIES FOR UNDUE INFLUENCE

If the above components are established, the victim is generally entitled to have the transaction set aside: *CIBC Mortgages plc* v *Pitt* [1994] 1 AC 200, HL. In reversing a transaction, the court will endeavour to return the parties to their original positions: *Cheese* v *Thomas* [1994] 1 All ER 35. If this is not possible, the court will look at all the circumstances to do what is fair and just in practical terms: *ibid*. In *Cheese* v *Thomas* the victim could not recover all the money which he had contributed to the purchase of a house since its value had diminished. Both parties shared in its reduced value; the defendant was not required to bear the entire burden of the fall in the property market.

*Note*, the doctrine gives a right to reverse a transaction only where purchasers for value in good faith without notice have not acquired rights in the subject matter of the transfer. The right to have a transaction set aside does not confer an interest in land but only a *mere equity*: as to the nature of which, see *National Provincial Bank Ltd* v *Ainsworth* [1965] AC 1175 at p. 1261. Such an equity is unlikely to suffice to give the victim of undue influence an overriding interest under LRA 1925, s. 70(1)(g), even where he is in actual occupation of the property mortgaged.

Where the transaction cannot be set aside the court can impose conditions to do justice as between the victim and lender: *Midland Bank plc* v *Greene* [1994] 2 FLR 827.

# FIVE

# ACQUIRING AN EQUITABLE INTEREST IN LAND

## 5.1 Generally

It is usually reasonably easy to ascertain who is or are the legal owners of land but it can be much more difficult to ascertain who are the equitable or beneficial owners and what are their respective shares and rights.

All property disputes between co-owners or alleged co-owners should be viewed against the background of the family jurisdiction of the courts. Where the co-owners are married, the courts have extensive discretionary powers to redistribute the property of the couple (see the **Family Law in Practice Manual**). The strict rules of property listed in this chapter are generally relevant to spouses only where one spouse becomes insolvent and the interests of the trustee in bankruptcy must be taken into account.

The courts' general powers to oust parties both from the matrimonial and quasi-matrimonial home may also need to be assessed in advising a cohabitee about remedies.

## 5.2 The Nature of Joint Ownership

Where the title deeds or land registration entry indicates that there is more than one owner of the property in question, there is a joint tenancy at law: LPA 1925, ss. 34(1) and 36(2). The equitable interest in such a property may be held by the co-owners as joint tenants or as tenants in common; in the latter case the parties hold undivided shares in the property. The joint tenancy will exist in equity as well as in law, only if:

(a)    the four unities are present, i.e., time, title, interest, possession;

(b)    there are no words of severance, e.g. 'equally', 'between' etc.;

(c)    no other circumstances exist indicating that a tenancy in common is intended, e.g., property held by partners.

### 5.2.1 THE RIGHT OF SURVIVORSHIP

Joint tenants are between them a single group owner of property; the owners are together entitled to the whole and no division is made. A joint tenant has no share to leave by will or intestacy. His share passes to the surviving joint tenants according to the *right of survivorship*. If the joint tenancy is severed in equity, the co-owners' shares pass on death according to their wills or the rules of intestate succession.

### 5.2.2 SEVERING THE JOINT TENANCY

Severance of a joint tenancy at law is not possible: LPA 1925, s. 36(2). A joint tenancy may be severed in equity:

(a)    by formal notice under LPA 1925, s. 36(2);

     (b)  under the rules in *Williams* v *Hensman* (1861) 1 John and H 546, 557:

        (i)  by the selling of a share by one co-owner;

        (ii)  by mutual agreement;

        (iii)  by a course of dealing between the co-owners sufficient to show an intention to treat themselves as owning separate shares.

An order made under the Administration of Insolvent Estates of Deceased Persons Order (SI 1986/1999) does not retrospectively sever the joint tenancy of the deceased's home: *Re Palmer* [1994] 3 All ER 835, CA.

## 5.3    Tenants in Common

### 5.3.1    ASSESSING THE PROPORTIONS IN WHICH THE PROPERTY IS HELD

If both the legal and the equitable interests in the property are held as a joint tenancy, no question of quantification arises, since the owners are together entitled to the whole (see **5.2.1**). If, however, the legal joint tenancy has been severed (see **5.2.2** for the means by which this is effected), the beneficial interest can be held in any proportions chosen by the parties to the resulting tenancy in common. The proportions may have been recorded in the conveyance or purchase deed entered into on acquisition of the property by the joint owners. With registered land, the proprietorship register should record the fact that the co-owners hold as tenants in common; it will not, however, specify the proportions in which the property is held; the registrar does not require co-owners to give such information. If good conveyancing practice has been followed, a separate deed or declaration, specifying the shares, will have been drawn up. In many cases, however, this will not have been done. If the parties simply intended to hold jointly, the court will generally presume that they intended to hold in equal shares: *Saville* v *Goodall* (1993) 25 HLR 588. See further **5.6**.

## 5.4    Trusts of Land

The procedure for applying for sale of all land held under the new trusts of land is regulated by ss. 14 and 15 of the Trusts of Land and Appointment of Trustees Act 1996. (On the relevance of the old law, see *TSB Bank plc* v *Marshall* (1998) CLY 502.)

### *Applications for order*
**14.**—*(1)  Any person who is a trustee of land or has an interest in property subject to a trust of land may make an application to the court for an order under this section.*

*(2)  On an application for an order under this section the court may make any such order—*

*    (a)  relating to the exercise by the trustees of any of their functions (including an order relieving them of any obligation to obtain the consent of, or to consult, any person in connection with the exercise of any of their functions), or*

*    (b)  declaring the nature or extent of a person's interest in property subject to the trust,*

*as the court thinks fit.*

*(3)  The court may not under this section make any order as to the appointment or removal of trustees.*

*(4)  The powers conferred on the court by this section are exercisable on an application whether it is made before or after the commencement of this Act.*

### *Matters relevant in determining applications*
**15.**—*(1)  The matters to which the court is to have regard in determining an application for an order under section 14 include—*

*    (a)  the intentions of the person or persons (if any) who created the trust,*

*    (b)  the purposes for which the property subject to the trust is held,*

> *(c)   the welfare of any minor who occupies or might reasonably be expected to occupy any land subject to the trust as his home, and*
> *(d)   the interests of any secured creditor of any beneficiary.*
> *(2)   In the case of an application relating to the exercise in relation to any land of the powers conferred on the trustees by section 13, the matters to which the court is to have regard also include the circumstances and wishes of each of the beneficiaries who is (or apart from any previous exercise by the trustees of those powers would be) entitled to occupy the land under section 12.*
> *(3)   In the case of any other application, other than one relating to the exercise of the power mentioned in section 6(2), the matters to which the court is to have regard also include the circumstances and wishes of any beneficiaries of full age and entitled to an interest in possession in property subject to the trust or (in case of dispute) of the majority (according to the value of their combined interests).*
> *(4)   This section does not apply to an application if section 335A of the Insolvency Act 1986 (which is inserted by Schedule 3 and relates to applications by a trustee of a bankrupt) applies to it.*

The guidelines in s. 15 are similar in effect to the body of case law interpreting the discretion given under the LPA 1925, s. 30. The earlier case law should, however, be treated with caution as under the old trust for sale there was a duty to sell and only a power to postpone whereas now the powers of sale and postponement are equally weighted.

If an application under s. 14 involves a trustee in bankruptcy, separate guidance applies by virtue of s. 335A(2) of the Insolvency Act 1986, which was inserted by the 1996 Act:

> *(1)   Any application by a trustee of a bankrupt's estate under section 14 of the Trusts of Land and Appointment of Trustees Act 1996 (powers of court in relation to trusts of land) for an order under that section for the sale of land shall be made to the court having jurisdiction in relation to the bankruptcy.*
> *(2)   On such an application the court shall make such order as it thinks just and reasonable having regard to—*
> *(a)   the interests of the bankrupt's creditors;*
> *(b)   where the application is made in respect of land which includes a dwelling house which is or has been the home of the bankrupt or the bankrupt's spouse or former spouse—*
> *(i)   the conduct of the spouse or former spouse, so far as contributing to the bankruptcy,*
> *(ii)   the needs and financial resources of the spouse or former spouse, and*
> *(iii)   the needs of any children; and*
> *(c)   all the circumstances of the case other than the needs of the bankrupt.*
> *(3)   Where such an application is made after the end of the period of one year beginning with the first vesting under Chapter IV of this Part of the bankrupt's estate in a trustee, the court shall assume, unless the circumstances of the case are exceptional, that the interests of the bankrupt's creditors outweigh all other considerations.*
> *(4)   The powers conferred on the court by this section are exercisable on an application whether it is made before or after the commencement of this section.*

### 5.4.1   PROTECTION FOR A PURCHASER

The purchaser should insist on payment to two trustees to take advantage of the overreaching provisions of LPA 1925, s. 27. This applies to the new trusts of land as well as trusts for sale. The only exception is where a sole surviving joint tenant conveys the property as a beneficial owner. To prevent an improper use of the statute, a joint owner who severs his interest should endorse this fact on the deeds or have a restriction placed on the land register. Where co-owners of registered land have indicated on a transfer that they intend to hold as tenants in common, a restriction will be placed on the proprietorship register: LRA 1925, s. 58(3). This serves as a warning to purchasers that a trust is in existence and that the appropriate steps should be taken.

Under the Trusts of Land and Appointment of Trustees Act 1996, s. 16(3), trustees are under a duty to take all reasonable steps to bring any restrictions to the notice of purchasers. But a purchaser is protected from any adverse consequences of the failure to obtain consents or comply with other restrictions imposed by s. 8 of the 1996 Act unless the purchaser has actual notice (s. 16(3)).

## 5.5 Acquisition of a Share in Land by Estoppel and/or Constructive Trust

Where property is registered in the name of a single cohabitee, the law will, in certain circumstances, hold that the property is held on trust, jointly for the legal owner and a cohabitee. An express written allocation of the beneficial interest will be conclusive; no contrary trust will be implied in such circumstances: *Goodman* v *Gallant* [1986] Fam 106. Most lenders will insist that all cohabitees sign a deed of release, acknowledging that they have no rights in the property.

Where the cohabitees have orally expressed an intention to hold the beneficial interest in certain shares, the courts may give effect to this intention by imposing a constructive trust. In order to succeed, a cohabitee must show that he has acted in reliance on the expression of intention. An oral agreement alone cannot suffice since it would not comply with the LPA 1925, s. 53. Qualifying acts include substantial indirect contributions by the claimant to a mortgage (e.g., contributions towards general household expenses; see *Grant* v *Edwards* [1986] Ch 638). The acts must be referable to the interest in the property. Mere decoration and supervision of renovation would be insufficient: *Lloyds Bank plc* v *Rosset* [1991] 1 AC 107 (they were acts which 'any wife' would do). Looking after children will not be sufficient on its own. Acting as an unpaid business associate has been held to be sufficient: *Hammond* v *Mitchell* [1991] 1 WLR 1127.

In certain circumstances, the court will imply a common intention to hold the property jointly, in the absence of an express declaration. Direct financial contributions to the purchase price of the land and/or mortgage repayments will constitute sufficient grounds to conclude that the requisite intention existed: see *Lloyds Bank plc* v *Rosset* [1991] 1 AC 107. 'It is at least extremely doubtful whether anything less will do' (*ibid.* at p. 133). Neither extensive work on the house nor substantial financial contributions to general household expenses will be sufficient for the court to imply an intention to own jointly.

### 5.5.1 PRACTICAL BARRIERS AND RELEVANT DOCUMENTS

The greatest practical barrier to establishing a constructive trust is proof of express joint intention. In most cases, the only available evidence will be your client's recollection of events leading up to the purchase of the house. The documents which should be checked include the deed of conveyance and any cohabitation or licence agreement which may have been entered into by the parties. The solicitors who dealt with the conveyance of the property may have attendance notes containing a useful indication of what the parties' intentions were. Many solicitors will specifically address the position of co-owners with those contemplating entering into a land transaction. Where the cohabitee has paid money directly towards the deposit and/or mortgage instalments, bank accounts should be examined for the relevant period. Similar issues may well arise where an estoppel is asserted.

### 5.5.2 PROCEDURE

If the co-owner seeking to establish the interest wishes the property to be sold, he may apply under the Trusts of Land and Appointment of Trustees Act 1996, s. 14. If the co-owner does not wish to sell, proceedings for a declaration may be issued. Formerly there was a choice between commencing with an originating summons or a writ. Now there is a choice between CPR, Part 8 and Part 7 style claim forms. It is likely that Part 8 will be more appropriate in most cases. The emphasis on early disclosure and early definition of the issues is likely to have a marked effect on cases in this area. Costs are likely to be run up at an earlier stage and although this may lead to more cases being settled, given the strength of feeling often engendered by these cases, it may have the effect of polarising the parties because once the costs have been incurred they have less to lose by fighting on.

## 5.6 Quantification of Interests of Co-owners under Constructive Trusts

Where a trust is imposed solely as a result of money contributions, quantification of interests will generally be in proportion to those contributions. Where the interest is based on implied intention coupled with detrimental reliance, the share granted is not necessarily proportionate to contributions and may be greater: e.g., *Grant* v *Edwards* [1986] Ch 638; *Saville* v *Goodall* (1993) 25 HLR 588, CA. The court will determine a fair division by taking a broad approach: *Gissing* v *Gissing* [1971] AC 886. Precise advice on the share to be expected is thus difficult. A claimant is entitled to a proportionate increase or decrease in the value of the share, brought about by fluctuations in the value of the property: *Turton* v *Turton* [1988] Ch 542. The time of acquisition is the relevant point, as far as ascertainment of shares is concerned, although later events can be taken into account: *Bernard* v *Josephs* [1982] Ch 391.

A co-owner may be ordered by the court to pay an occupation rent to a fellow co-owner no longer living in the premises. Such an order will be made where it is necessary to do equity between the parties. Such a necessity will arise in, but is not confined to, the situation where one co-owner has been excluded by the other from the property: *Re Pavlou* [1993] 1 WLR 1046.

## 5.7 Proprietary Estoppel

A cohabitee, X, may be able to establish a proprietary estoppel against the owner of property, Y, if the following can be shown:

(a) Detriment, which generally includes expenditure; the expenditure need not have been on Y's property; work on X's property suffices if it was done in the expectation of being granted some right over that of Y: *Snell's Equity*, 29th edn, 1990, at p. 574. Other detriment which suffices includes:

    (i) acting as an unpaid housekeeper and later mistress to Y: *Pascoe* v *Turner* [1979] 1 WLR 431;

    (ii) cohabiting with the son of and nursing the daughter of Y: *Greasley* v *Cooke* [1980] 1 WLR 1306.

(b) An expectation or belief on the part of X that X will acquire a sufficient interest in Y's property to justify the expenditure, or other detriment. Expenditure in the mere hope of such an interest, where X takes a risk on its refusal, is insufficient: *Snell* at p. 575.

(c) Encouragement by Y, either actively or by standing by with the knowledge that X is incurring the expenditure on the grounds of the belief set out above. Y must know of not only the expenditure and belief, but also of Y's own rights in the relevant property: *Snell*, p. 576.

### 5.7.1    REMEDIES FOR SATISFYING THE EQUITY

The remedy for satisfying the equity in cases of proprietary estoppel is at the discretion of the court. It is thus dependent on the individual circumstances of the case and the courts have been very flexible. Examples of remedies conferred include:

(a) An equitable lien on the property for the extent of the expenditure: *Hussey* v *Palmer* [1972] 1 WLR 1286. Alternatively, possession may be ordered conditionally on Y repaying the cost of the improvements made: *Dodsworth* v *Dodsworth* (1973) 228 EG 1115.

(b) Legal title to the property, even where the expenditure is not substantial: *Pascoe* v *Turner* [1979] 1 WLR 431.

(c) A licence to occupy for a certain period or for life. Note the potential effect of the Settled Land Act 1925 in such cases (see **1.5.3**).

In many cases, estoppel will be pleaded as well as, or in the alternative to, a constructive or resulting trust. The facts giving rise to estoppels often appear to have little to distinguish them from the trusts cases. A plea of estoppel has the advantage of the wider range of remedies.

## 5.8    Interests Falling Short of Co-ownership

Where neither an interest in land nor an estoppel can be established, the cohabitee is likely to be a mere licensee. Licensees have extremely limited rights (see **5.9** below).

## 5.9    Licences

### 5.9.1    INTRODUCTION

A licence cannot strictly create a proprietary interest in land; it represents simply a permission to enter land where entry would otherwise constitute trespass. The degree to which a licence may be enforced depends upon the nature of the licence.

Generally most attempts to create a licence to evade the statutory protection of tenants under the Rent Acts and Housing Acts will be ineffective and will create a lease if exclusive possession is given to the tenant: *Street* v *Mountford* [1985] AC 809, HL. Licences may be created if exclusive possession is not given: *AG Securities* v *Vaughan* [1990] 1 AC 417.

### 5.9.2    BARE LICENCES

A bare licence is a licence that is granted without consideration passing. It may be granted expressly or by implication; an unlocked front garden gate amounts to an implied licence to members of the public to approach the front door of a house in the course of their lawful business: *Robson* v *Hallet* [1967] 2 QB 939.

A bare licence may be revoked by the licensor at will, although the licensee may have a reasonable time to leave the premises: *Robson* v *Hallet*. In the case of a bare licence to occupy premises granted under a 'family arrangement' such a reasonable time may be anything up to 12 months: *E & L Berg Homes Ltd* v *Grey* (1980) 253 EG 473.

### 5.9.3    LICENCES COUPLED WITH A GRANT

When someone is granted the right to remove something from the land of another, as, for example, in the case of a profit à prendre, an ancillary licence will also be created to enable that person to enter the land to remove that to which he is entitled. A licence coupled with the grant of an interest is valid provided that the interest to which it attached is properly created.

Such a licence is irrevocable at common law so long as the interest to which it is coupled subsists. It is therefore binding on third parties and may also be assigned together with the proprietary interest.

### 5.9.4 CONTRACTUAL LICENCES

A contractual licence, granted for consideration, is generally enforceable according to the terms of the contract which are determined by the usual contractual principles. Terms may therefore be implied in the licence, e.g. for quiet enjoyment and fitness for purpose: *Smith* v *Nottinghamshire County Council* (1981) *The Times*, 13 November 1981.

It was thought that a contractual licence could be revoked at any time without recourse by the licensee save damages for breach of contract; on this basis a contractual licence could not be enforced against a third party. In the context of a licence to reside in a house, it was held in *Errington* v *Errington and Woods* [1952] 1 KB 290 that such a licence could be enforced against a third party with superior title. However, this view has been rejected, *obiter*, by the Court of Appeal in *Ashburn Anstalt* v *Arnold* [1989] Ch 1. It appears that the ordinary rules of privity will apply, at least until the House of Lords gives a definitive ruling.

In the context of a 'periodic licence' of a dwelling it should be noted that such a licence can only be terminated on four weeks' notice in writing: Protection from Eviction Act 1977, s. 5(1A), as amended by the Housing Act 1988. 'Periodic licence' is not defined in the 1977 Act, but in *Norris* v *Checksfield* [1991] 1 WLR 1241 the Court of Appeal interpreted it as being an analogy with a weekly, monthly or quarterly tenancy.

### 5.9.5 LICENCES COUPLED WITH AN EQUITY

The courts may in certain circumstances grant equitable relief to prevent a licensor revoking a contractual licence where it would be inequitable to do so on the grounds of promissory estoppel: *Greasley* v *Cooke* [1980] 1 WLR 1346. It has been suggested that they are enforceable against third parties who are on notice: *ER Ives Investments* v *High* [1967] 2 QB 379, but this case may be interpreted in other ways; the original licence conferred a benefit on the licensor as well as the licensee, which it would be inequitable for the licensor's successors in title to enjoy without bearing the burden of the licence as well.

More recently the Court of Appeal has appeared to indicate that a contractual licence is not generally binding on a third party, although there may be certain occasions where a licence may be enforced against third parties by means of a constructive trust: *Ashburn Anstalt* v *Arnold* [1989] Ch 1.

# SIX

# EXPRESS TRUSTS AND TESTAMENTARY DISPOSITIONS

## 6.1    Introduction

Problems relating to express trusts and wills can present themselves in a great variety of ways. An individual may seek advice on making provision for his family and dependants. Provision may be made simply by drawing up a will or by making gifts during life, or a combination of both. Choices have to be made whether outright gifts will be appropriate, or some kind of trust. Insurance cover may also need to be considered. In most cases, a solicitor will give advice and draft appropriate documents, often using or adapting standard forms for wills, trusts and deeds of gift. Counsel's advice may be sought on drafting a particularly difficult clause, or where there is some complication in the facts of the case. Very careful consideration of the relevant tax provisions is necessary in giving advice and drafting the documents, or parts of them, in this area. After a will or a trust has been set up, executors or trustees may seek advice either because there is doubt about who they should distribute property to, or what property is available, or there is some difficulty with the interpretation or scope of their administrative powers. There may be a pre-existing dispute with beneficiaries, or potential beneficiaries, but often the executors or trustees are seeking clarification before any dispute arises. On the death of an individual, members of the family or dependants may seek advice regarding their entitlement. Their provision will depend primarily on the provisions of any will, or on the rules of intestacy. If these do not make sufficient provision, the individual may be able to make an application to court for an order for provision under the Inheritance (Provision for Family and Dependants) Act 1975. Disgruntled beneficiaries, or would-be beneficiaries, may also seek advice about the interpretation of a will or trust, or about the management of a trust by the trustees.

## 6.2    Creation of Express Trusts

There are two ways of creating an express trust obligation: (1) by declaration of oneself as trustee of specified property; (2) by intention to create a trust, coupled with transfer to trustees. Formalities are only required for trusts of land and testamentary dispositions. However, many trusts are set up by deed.

## 6.3    Deeds

A deed is a formal document used for transactions which the law regards as particularly serious. Its structure is formal but largely governed by convention. Deeds are normally divided into three parts:

(a)    introduction;

(b)    recitals;

(c)    operative part.

Until the advent of the typewriter (about the time of the First World War), and now the word processor, deeds were copied by hand in copperplate lettering. Various different 'palaeographical' styles were used to act as punctuation marks to delineate the boundaries of the various clauses. The writing in deeds and suchlike documents had to fill the entire parchment to prevent fraudulent alterations or additions. Capitals, underlining and interspacing are the modern equivalent of these 'palaeographical' styles. Their precise use is a matter of individual taste, but the examples used in this Manual are thought to be reasonably representative. Modern deeds are normally double spaced and a line is drawn from the end of each paragraph to the right-hand margin to prevent interpolations or additions.

It remains to be seen how far the facilities for different fonts which are now available on the more advanced word processors lead to an increased use of the different 'palaeographical' styles. Certainly some engrossers are already emboldening, for example, the parties' names.

Counsel drafting a deed (or other legal document) for a solicitor will often use square brackets. These are used in three situations by lawyers:

(a)  as part of the citation of cases;

(b)  when making an interpolation in a quotation; and

(c)  when drafting a legal document, where something has to be filled in by the person who is to engross the document, e.g. 'Bilbo Baggins of [address]'.

**6.3.1      PARTS OF A DEED**

**6.3.1.1      Introduction**
The first part of a deed is the introduction. It says what the deed is, gives the date of and the parties to the deed. The opening words say what type of deed it is, and up to 1926 these had to be right. Now this matters less because the Law of Property Act 1925 (LPA 1925), s. 57 provides that it is no longer necessary to describe a deed as an indenture, even if it is one. A deed is usually described as what it is, e.g. THIS CONVEYANCE, THIS LEASE, THIS MORTGAGE, or (if there is nothing better) simply THIS DEED. Notice how the description of the deed is conventionally put in capital letters and often underlined.

It may be that the word 'Deed' here will be used more often, to ensure that the deed complies with the requirement of s. 1(2)(a) of the Law of Property (Miscellaneous Provisions) Act 1989 that a deed must make it clear on its face that it is a deed '(whether by describing itself as a deed or expressing itself to be executed or signed as a deed or otherwise)'. Time will tell, but it seems likely that the other possible methods will find more favour as it is clearly useful to know what type of deed one is dealing with (conveyance, lease etc). As we shall see, the testatum always describes the document as a deed.

In practice one sometimes has to look at old deeds. An indenture is a deed with more than one party to it — so called because the deed was copied out in parallel as many times as there were parties and then cut into that many parts (hence the term party). The cuts 'indented' the deed, which could then be put together again to prove that each part was still the same. A deed with only one party is called a deed poll, 'poll' being the Norman French word for smooth — because it was not cut and indented.

The true date of a deed is the date of delivery. It is presumed that the date on the face of a deed is the date from which it is effective, i.e. the date of delivery. This presumption is rebuttable by proof that the date of delivery was some other date. Deeds are usually dated with the date of completion of the transaction, not the earlier date (if any) of actual execution. When a deed is engrossed, the day and the month are usually left blank to be inserted in manuscript on delivery (which has to await signature by all parties, often separately). Solicitors circulating a deed for execution usually pencil in the words 'do not date'.

To be a party to a deed, a person must be specified as such; merely being mentioned in a deed does not make someone a party. Neither does executing it. Who needs to be a party to a given deed depends on the circumstances, but anyone who is to be bound by the deed must be a party.

The whole introduction looks like this:

THIS DEED is made the [ .. ] day of [ ........ ] 1993 BETWEEN BILBO BAGGINS of Bag End Hobbiton in the County of Shire (hereinafter called "the Donor") of the one part and FRODO BAGGINS of 1 Bag Lane Hobbiton as aforesaid (hereinafter called "the Donee") of the other part.

### 6.3.1.2 Recitals

The recitals begin with the word 'WHEREAS:—', which is normally in capital letters and often interspaced and underlined.

In days gone by recitals were usually very long, but nowadays they tend to be kept as short as possible. Transfer forms under registered conveyancing have no recitals since only the Chief Land Registrar sees them, and therefore recitals would be otiose.

If a deed is expressed to be supplemental to another deed, the whole of that other deed is deemed to have been recited in the first deed: LPA 1925, s. 58.

There are two types of recital:

(a) Narrative recitals: these set out the facts and the instruments necessary to show the vendor's title, the terms of the will and devolution in a deed of family arrangement, the right to make such an appointment in an appointment of a new trustee, etc. Further examples are the sole surviving joint tenant's recital and the personal representatives' s. 36 recital.

(b) Introductory recitals: these explain the purpose of the deed (e.g. the recital of an agreement for sale, the reason for the deed of family arrangement).

Recitals can have various effects:

(a) They can create estoppels, because an executing party is bound by a recital of a specific fact in an action founded on the deed. The estoppel operates in favour of those who are intended to and do act on the deed. So if a grantor recites a given title, he cannot deny it. Thus if by any means the grantor subsequently acquires the title (which he did not have at the date of the deed), that title will pass by the estoppel without a confirmatory conveyance: *Cumberland Court (Brighton) Ltd* v *Taylor* [1964] Ch 29. This is called 'feeding the estoppel'.

(b) They can be evidence, since recitals in a deed 20 years old are sufficient evidence of their truth until proved inaccurate: LPA 1925, s. 45(6). Recitals in a deed appointing new trustees of land declaring the reason for the vacancy giving rise to the new appointment must be accepted by a purchaser as conclusive evidence of what is stated: the Trustee Act 1925, s. 38 and the Settled Land Act 1925, s. 35(3).

(c) Recitals by a personal representative under s. 36(6) of the Administration of Estates Act 1925 are useful and very important.

(d) They are a statutory declaration so that making a false recital is perjury.

(e) Recitals can occasionally create covenants. Because no special or technical form of words is required to create a covenant, a recital showing the intention of one of the parties to do or not to do something will create a covenant to or not to do that thing unless the deed expresses a contrary intention.

(f) Recitals can help to construe the deed: *Re Moon* (1886) 17 QBD 275, 286 where it was held that:

(i) if the operative part is ambiguous, then clear recitals will govern the construction of the deed;

(ii) if the recitals are ambiguous, then a clear operative part will govern;

(iii) if both are clear but inconsistent, the operative part will govern.

### 6.3.1.3 Operative part

The testatum is the words which introduce the operative part. It is customarily as follows:

NOW THIS DEED WITNESSETH as follows:—

These words are normally in capital letters and often underlined. Some draftsmen prefer the modern form 'WITNESSES', but the older form 'WITNESSETH' is still common. Though it is hallowed by the Authorised Version of the Bible, it in fact derives from the Anglo-Saxon third-person singular ending.

As its name suggests, the operative part is the portion of the deed which actually effectuates the purpose of the deed. After the testatum it usually begins with the words 'Pursuant to' or 'In pursuance of' and then either 'the said agreement' or 'the said desire' or as appropriate, depending on why the deed is being made and thus what has been recited.

The deed then proceeds as a series of numbered clauses. The last of these, the certificate for value, is needed for stamp duty purposes where the value of the consideration is below the threshold for stamp duty (currently £60,000). The formula is as follows:

It is hereby certified that the transaction hereby effected does not form part of a larger transaction or a series of transactions in respect of which the amount or value of the consideration exceeds £60,000.

This prevents a transaction being fragmented to avoid stamp duty.

A conveyance for valuable consideration is liable for stamp duty. The current rate is 1 per cent if the consideration is over £60,000. There is no stamp duty if the consideration is under that amount, but stamp duty is charged on a 'slab principle' rather than a 'slice principle', so there is no marginal relief. If the consideration is £60,001, £601 in stamp duty is payable.

The recipient is responsible for having the conveyance stamped and there are penalties for being late. Once the conveyance is executed it must be stamped within 30 days: Stamp Act 1891. Provided it is lodged with the stamping office by then, that suffices.

A new form of certificate has recently been introduced for certain categories of instrument now exempt from stamp duty (e.g. gifts *inter vivos*, appointments of new trustees). Here the formula is: 'It is hereby certified that this instrument falls within Category [L] in the Schedule to the Stamp Duty (Exempt Instruments) Regulations 1987.' These regulations list the exempt categories.

### 6.3.1.4 Testimonium

The clause which links the signatures and (before 31 July 1990) the seals to the rest of the document is called the 'testimonium' (from the Latin words with which it formerly began, *in cuius rei testimonium*). Its omission will not invalidate the document and it is unnecessary (and does not usually appear) in instruments dealing with registered land. But apart from this it should never be omitted in practice as it preserves evidence of due execution and is thus important.

The form of the testimonium for deeds delivered before 31 July 1990 is as follows:

IN WITNESS whereof the parties hereto have hereunto set their hands and seals the day and year first above written

For instruments delivered as deeds on or after 31 July 1990, this needs to be modified as follows:

IN WITNESS whereof this instrument has been duly executed as a deed by the parties hereto the day and year first above written.

The words 'IN WITNESS' tend to be in capitals and underlined. This is the form for deeds under seal. For documents merely under hand the formula is 'AS WITNESS the hands of the parties hereto'. For a will the formula is 'IN WITNESS whereof I have hereunto set my hand this [..] day of [......] 19[..]'. The distinction between the use of IN WITNESS and AS WITNESS is of no legal significance and purely a matter of practice. Counsel when drafting a document customarily abbreviates the testimonium to 'IN WITNESS etc' or 'AS WITNESS etc.', as appropriate.

The customary form of attestation (for deeds delivered before 31 July 1990) is as follows:

SIGNED SEALED AND DELIVERED
by the said Bilbo Baggins
in the presence of

                                                                                              L. S.

For instruments delivered as deeds on or after 31 July 1990, this needs to be modified as follows:—

SIGNED [AND DELIVERED] AS A DEED
by the above-named [name]
in the presence of
(Signature, name and address
of attesting witness]

Following the case of *Venetian Glass Galleries Ltd* v *Next Properties Ltd* [1989] 2 EGLR 42 it is thought that the words '[AND DELIVERED]' should only be included where the deed is to be effective immediately on signing or as an escrow.

Unlike a will, there was no legal requirement that the execution of a deed be witnessed. Provided it was executed by all the relevant parties it was fully binding. In practice each executing party normally had one witness to his signature. There was then someone to prove due execution if necessary. The witnesses put their signatures, names, addresses and occupations under the words 'in the presence of' and by the left-hand margin. The parties executed the deed with their signatures and seals towards the right-hand margin. A transfer of land has always needed to be attested under the Land Registry Rules 1926. However, deeds executed on or after 31 July 1990 must, under the 1989 Act, be attested by at least one witness.

Before 1926 a deed had to be sealed with real sealing wax, but did not have to be signed. This practice went back to medieval times, when a precursor of sealing was signing one's name beside a Greek cross (+), which was regarded as more holy and binding — compare how bishops still sign their names today. Now the law has come almost full circle. Since 1925 a deed had to be signed as well as sealed and delivered: LPA 1925, s. 73(1). Since 1925 the seal has been a wafer seal rather than sealing wax. Indeed the Court of Appeal has decided that if the letters 'L.S.' (*locus sigilli*, place of the seal) appear in a circle where the wafer seal should go, that suffices to seal the document: *First National Securities Ltd* v *Jones* [1978] Ch 109. Sir David Cairns said *obiter* in that case that merely signing by the words 'signed sealed and delivered' sufficed to seal it. Many people of late used one or other of these methods of sealing.

This case generated some looseness of practice in sealing documents. The present attitude of the courts is to be stricter and not to say that the document is actually sealed but to regard the party who only uses 'signed sealed and delivered' as estopped from denying sealing: *TCB Ltd* v *Gray* [1986] Ch 621, 633 per Sir Nicolas Browne-Wilkinson V-C.

Since 31 July 1990 (when s. 1 of the Law of Property (Miscellaneous Provisions) Act 1989 came into force), the law has come full circle. Section 73 of the LPA 1925 is repealed and deeds executed by individuals no longer need sealing. To be a deed, an instrument now has to:

(a) make it clear on its face that it is intended to be a deed, e.g. by describing itself as a deed or by expressing itself to be executed and signed as a deed;

(b) be validly executed as a deed.

To be so validly executed the deed has to be signed, witnessed (by one witness) and delivered. Thus signing alone replaces signing and sealing. Remember that signing is really a modern equivalent of sealing. Witnessing has become a legal requirement. Delivery is still required. Section 1 applies only to deeds executed by individuals, and not by corporations (even corporations sole) or to deeds actually delivered before it came into force.

However, s. 36A of the Companies Act 1985 (added by s. 130 of the Companies Act 1989) enables a company registered under the Act (acting through its secretary or director(s)) to execute deeds delivered on or after 31 July 1990 without sealing, if it so wishes.

Where someone executes a deed in two capacities, it is easiest to sign twice, because it is easier to prove then that the execution was intended to cover all the capacities in which that party had to execute the deed.

If a party is to be bound by a deed, that party must execute it. But someone can take the benefit of a deed without executing it. If so, that party will be bound by any condition in the deed, despite not executing it: *Elliston* v *Reacher* [1908] 2 Ch 665.

A purchaser must execute a deed if it contains purchaser's covenants or a declaration of two or more purchasers' beneficial interests. Execution by the purchaser is not necessary merely because the vendor reserves an easement: LPA 1925, s. 65(1).

## 6.3.2 DELIVERY OF A DEED

Delivery of a deed is any act done with the intention to be bound; it can be actual or constructive. Actual delivery is where the document is actually delivered into another's custody. Constructive delivery is where the deed is executed with the intention that it shall be the irrevocable deed of the maker.

Delivery can also be absolute or conditional. The former means that the deed comes into immediate effect. A deed conditionally delivered is called an escrow and only becomes operative when the relevant event happens (e.g., payment of purchase moneys, or delivery of the counterpart). A deed cannot be made conditional on the grantor's death, because a testamentary disposition requires the formalities of a will. An escrow commits the grantor irrevocably and remains effective despite his intervening death: *Perryman's Case* (1599) 5 Co Rep 84a. In a normal sale of land transaction, the vendor will execute the conveyance and entrust it to his solicitor to be given to the purchaser on completion. Here the court will infer an intention that delivery is conditional on the payment of the purchase moneys and (where appropriate) execution by the purchaser: *Glessing* v *Green* [1975] 2 All ER 696; cf. *Venetian Glass Galleries Ltd* v *Next Properties Ltd* [1989] 2 EGLR 42 (Harman J) (formal licence to assign a lease which had been engrossed and sealed held to be an escrow conditional on delivery of the counterpart and the payment of certain moneys). Although this practice may obtain on the grant of a lease, normally and particularly where the negotiations have all been 'subject to contract', the court will treat the lease and counterpart not as escrows upon signing (and sealing) but as being transmuted from mere pieces of paper (or parchment) into a fully fledged legally binding deed on (and only on) exchange, so that neither party is bound at all until exchange: *Longman* v *Viscount Chelsea* (1989) 58 P & CR 189. In the course of a conveyancing transaction, solicitors, licensed conveyancers, and their agents or employees are conclusively presumed, in favour of a purchaser, to be authorised to deliver as a deed an instrument on behalf of a party: s. 1(5) of the Law of Property (Miscellaneous Provisions) Act 1989. An escrow can be put in writing.

When the condition is fulfilled the deed takes effect from the date of the original delivery. So the legal estate is passed retrospectively, but this confers no right to the intermediate rents, nor does it validate a notice to quit given by the grantee between the actual date of delivery and the date of fulfilment: *Thompson* v *McCullough* [1947] KB 447. In *Alan Estates Ltd* v *W. G. Stores Ltd* [1982] Ch 511 a lease was delivered as an escrow; the conditions were satisfied 18 days later. The rent was payable 'from the date hereof'. The Court of Appeal held that because the term of an undated lease under seal begins at the date of delivery, rent was payable from the original delivery and not from the later date on which the conditions were satisfied.

For stamp duty purposes the operative date is when the escrow is satisfied, usually the date of actual completion on payment of the purchase price. Therefore that is the proper date for insertion in the deed: *Terrapin International Ltd* v *IRC* [1976] 1 WLR 665.

Where a deed is not to be delivered on signing, it may be that draftsmen will want to emphasise this by beginning the deed 'THIS [CONVEYANCE] delivered as a deed on the . . . . day of . . . . . . . 19 . .'.

If a deed has several parties, then it is immediately binding, unless it is executed in escrow, with the intention that the executing party will not be bound unless and until all the other parties execute it: *Naas* v *Westminster Bank Ltd* [1940] AC 366.

## 6.3.3 TRUST INSTRUMENTS

The Settled Land Act 1925 requires that strict settlements must be created by two documents. Trusts for sale were historically created by two documents, one expounding the trusts and the other conveying the land. Indeed, this is where the framers of the Settled Land Act 1925 found the idea. A trust of land can still be created *inter vivos* by this means, and this is done where the trusts are complicated. Where the trusts are simple and succinct this is unnecessary and one document suffices. Where there is a will there are *ipso facto* two documents — the will and assent vesting the property in the trustees. So also when shares or the like are to be transferred. Quite often assets are transferred to trustees after the execution of the trust instrument.

Trust instruments follow the pattern of other deeds. The settlor and the trustees are the normal parties. The recitals normally recite the desire to make and the reasons for making the settlement (e.g., to provide for the settlor's children or grandchildren). The conveyance or transfer of the property and the likelihood of further transfers will normally be recited too. The operative part sets out the trusts.

Normally clause 1 of the operative part is the definitions clause. It sets out all the terms which are to be used in a special sense in that deed with their respective meanings. It is a good idea to give each defined term an initial capital letter, e.g., 'the Trust Fund', so that it is clear to the reader at a glance that it is a defined term throughout the document. Clause 2 will then create the trust for sale. Then the trusts themselves will be set out, and a typical layout for these would be:

(a) power to appoint (often effectively a power to rewrite the trusts themselves, if not the whole settlement);

(b) discretionary power to apply income to minor children;

(c) trust for accumulation for 21 years or (if sooner) when the minors all come of age;

(d) income to the adult beneficiaries until, say, 25;

(e) distribution of capital, say, to all those beneficiaries attaining 25;

(f) ultimate remainder.

This last is important, as the trust property will revert back to the settlor if the trust provisions fail. This can have adverse tax implications in that it may well render the settlement ineffective for the purposes of mitigating (or avoiding) tax. Quite often a charity is chosen as the ultimate beneficiary. Of course if everything is distributed under its discretionary powers or the other trusts, the remainderman gets nothing.

This may be followed by a power to advance capital. Sections 31 and 32 of the Trustee Act 1925 are implied into all trust instruments unless there is a contrary intention. It is sensible drafting practice to provide specifically that they shall apply, or that they shall not apply (as desired), then there is no room for argument. Remember that s. 32 does not apply to a beneficiary whose only interest is in income. A special and express power is needed if capital is to be advanced to such a beneficiary.

Normally the investment clause will follow. Although the Trustee Investments Act 1961 considerably widened the powers of investment given to trustees by statute, it is normal practice nowadays to widen their powers still further, even to the extent of giving them power to invest as if they were beneficial owners absolutely entitled. The more relaxed attitude of the courts to investment powers is displayed in the case of *Trustees of the British Museum* v *A-G* [1984] 1 WLR 418. There are currently proposals to repeal the Trustee Investments Act 1961 leaving beneficiaries' interests to be protected by the law on trustees' fiduciary duties and the financial services legislation. To date, the required order under the Deregulation and Contracting Out Act 1994 has not yet been made.

After this any special powers can be granted. Practice varies here, some draftsmen tending to give more powers than others. The important thing is to ensure that the trustees will have all the powers they need to run the settlement in the way in which it is desired that they do so. Powers are also necessary for the protection of the trustees. For example, a '*Re Macadam* clause' is often inserted to enable trustees to use trust shares to qualify them to act as directors and keep any remuneration they earn for acting as such. Often nowadays a trustees' remuneration clause is inserted to enable professional trustees (or a trust corporation) to be appointed a trustee of the settlement and to be paid for acting. Normally professional people and trust corporations will not act as trustees gratis! Without such a clause (or a court order) trustees are strictly forbidden by equity from being paid, unless the beneficiaries are all *sui juris* and agree. With one it may be possible to obtain the services of a trustee who is able to do a much better job for the beneficiaries.

Often, too, a clause is inserted to exonerate trustees from liability for breach of trust other than wilful fraud or wrongdoing. Opinions vary as to the desirability of inserting such a clause. Certainly specific instructions should be taken before inserting such a clause. It has the merit of protecting lay trustees, who often commit unwitting breaches of trust in total ignorance of what they are doing and with the best intentions towards the beneficiaries. This may be felt better than leaving them to rely on the protection of the Trustee Act 1925, s. 61 (power of the court to exonerate trustees in proper cases). Professional trustees tend to like such a clause, not merely out of legitimate self-interest, but because their professional indemnity insurance policies do not always cover this type of work. It is submitted, however, that such clauses are undesirable, quite unnecessary and inimical to the beneficiaries' interests in the case of a trust corporation and the court is likely to construe them restrictively. (See *Armitage* v *Nurse* [1997] 2 All ER 705 and *Wight* v *Olswang* (1998) *The Times*, 18 May 1999, CA.)

## 6.3.4    VESTING DEED

A vesting deed will normally be a conveyance or transfer of the property to the trustees. With settled land it must contain the particulars set out in the Settled Land Act 1925, s. 5(1).

If the vendors are to hold on trust, this is normally stated in the habendum, e.g. 'TO HOLD unto the purchasers in fee simple UPON TRUST to sell the same (with full power to postpone the sale) and to stand possessed of the net proceeds of sale and pending sale any net profits in trust for themselves as tenants in common'. Alternatively, this can be expressed as a separate clause, e.g. 'The Purchasers shall stand possessed of the property hereby conveyed UPON TRUST etc.'. This is the shorter form commonly used to create a trust for sale and is perfectly adequate where the trusts are a simple declaration, effectively, of the statutory trusts. The rest of the trusts and powers can be left to be implied by statute. Indeed the formula 'TO HOLD unto the Purchasers as joint tenants [/as tenants in common]' is commonly used, leaving all the trusts and powers to be so implied.

Where the trusts are more complicated and a separate deed is needed, the conveyance would normally read 'TO HOLD unto the Purchasers upon the trusts of a trust instrument bearing even date herewith and executed immediately before this deed'. The expression 'bearing even date herewith' is the customary expression meaning 'on the same day as'.

Where the land is conveyed to five or more people, the legal estate can only be vested in a maximum of four of them. If the conveyance purports to vest it in more than four, it will only operate to vest the legal estate in the first four named. So the purchasers should choose in advance in which four people they wish the property to be vested. Where this happens, the four holding the legal estate have it vested in them on the statutory trusts.

## 6.3.5    DEEDS OF FAMILY ARRANGEMENT

Deeds of family arrangement (DoFAs) are currently very popular in practice. Strictly speaking they are deeds which rearrange a family's property, say, to preserve the family honour. Often, though, the term is used for what are more strictly deeds of variation which merely rearrange the dispositions under someone's will. There may be many reasons why a will does not make adequate provision for family and dependants. For example, the testator may have been ill for a long time and thus unable to alter the will to take account of recent developments in the family saga. The family may have wanted to do something different all along but may have been unwilling to tell poor old Uncle George that this was so. There may be an ambiguity in the will or in a chain of title which needs resolving or the testator may simply have done things in a tax-inefficient way.

Basically a DoFA simply rewrites the will. The parties to it have to be the personal representatives of the deceased and all those beneficiaries who are affected by the rearrangement. Otherwise they will not be bound. It is important to remember that a DoFA cannot be made where there are minor beneficiaries, because they cannot execute a deed and be bound by it until they reach 18. If a rewriting of the will is necessary and the beneficiaries are not of age (or unascertainable or unborn) the court can be asked to consent on their behalf on an application under the Variation of Trusts Act 1958. In theory all the beneficiaries signing the deed must receive independent advice to prevent them trying at a later date to upset the DoFA on the basis of undue influence. In practice, however, such beneficiaries very often object to taking such advice on the grounds that they know what they want to do and do not want to pay extra to have it pointed out to them that they are making a gift. The important thing from the lawyer's point of view, though, is that the advice (and warning) to take independent advice be given, and that this fact be recorded in writing. This can require due tact and diplomacy on the part of the adviser.

The recitals generally set out the will of the testator, the death and the grant of representation. It is often sensible to recite the fact that the beneficiaries are all those who on any view are entitled to the estate and are all absolutely so entitled. A recital that the beneficiaries have received (or at least been advised to take) independent advice is sensible.

The operative part starts by setting out the desired rewriting of the will. It should also include suitable clauses of release and indemnity. The trustees are technically acting in breach of trust in that they are not carrying out the instructions of the trust instrument (usually the will) and therefore they need a release. The deed then acts as an estoppel by deed (which is a good reason for using a deed). The indemnities give protection if a claim is subsequently made, and their presence is another reason why it is desirable that the beneficiaries have independent advice. People are often quite happy to sign guarantees, indemnities and the like without realising that they could incur liability under them and actually have to pay out money.

# 6.4 Wills

## 6.4.1 FORMAL REQUIREMENTS

There are innumerable ways of setting out the provisions of and arranging the clauses of a will, but very few of these have ever had any adverse effect on the validity of the will as a whole or of any disposition contained in it. An arrangement involving non-compliance with the provision in the Wills Act 1837, s. 9 as originally enacted, which required signature of the will by the testator 'at the foot or end thereof', would have invalidated a will. Even after the relaxation brought about by the Wills Act Amendment Act 1852, a signature could not operate to effectuate any part of the will which was underneath the signature or followed it in space. Although the courts tended to interpret the 1852 Act as leniently as possible (*Re Roberts* [1934] P 102; *In the Goods of Hornby* [1946] P 171), a will was declared invalid in a case where the testatrix signed her name at the top because there was no room at the bottom: *Re Stalman* (1931) 145 LT 339. However, in the case of deaths after 31 December 1982, the applicable provision is amended by the Administration of Justice Act 1982, s. 17, so that the test is now whether the will was in writing and signed by the testator and the testator intended by his signature to give effect to the will. Thus, in the present state of the law, a will could begin with the testimonium if the maker so desired: see *Wood* v *Smith* [1993] Ch 90. The choice between the innumerable arrangements alluded to above is therefore to be made without reference to formal requirements, but by considering which arrangement will render the will most easily intelligible to those who will be concerned with or affected by it.

Under the Wills Act 1837, s. 9 a will must be signed by the testator and witnesses in the presence of each other. A lenient interpretation was used in *Couser* v *Couser* [1996] 1 WLR 1301 to validate a will where a witness had signed earlier but acknowledged her signature in the presence of the testator and other witnesses.

## 6.4.2 VESTING OF PROPERTY ON DEATH — DUTIES OF EXECUTORS

On death, the real and personal estate of the testator or testatrix vests in an executor or executrix appointed by the will, provided that the executor or executrix (if a natural person) is of full age and has the capacity to manage his affairs. (Part I of the Administration of Estates Act 1925 (AEA 1925) deals with the devolution of real estate, which is defined in s. 3 of that Act.) Persons so appointed by the testator are very often appointed 'executor and trustee', though, in some cases, trustees may be appointed who are not the same persons as the executors. Unless the only dispositions in the will are immediate absolute gifts, it is advisable to provide for both offices to be filled. This is because the functions of executors and of trustees are quite distinct. Broadly speaking, the executor is concerned with winding up the estate and distributing assets, whereas a trustee has to retain assets until some specified event occurs. The duties of an executor can be summarised as follows:

(a) To collect in the real and personal estate of the deceased and administer it according to law.

(b) To take reasonable care to preserve the value of the estate.

(c) To ascertain and pay debts and liabilities of the deceased which are properly payable out of the assets in hand properly available for the purpose, including agreement of the liability of the deceased for income tax, capital gains tax and inheritance tax at the time of death. The order in which the assets of a solvent estate are to be applied to the payment of debts is governed by AEA 1925, s. 34(3) and sch. 1, part II. Where the estate is insolvent, the order of priority of debts is regulated by the Administration of Insolvent Estates of Deceased Persons Order 1986 (SI 1986/1999).

(d) To exhibit on oath a full inventory of the estate, when required by the court to do so, and to render an account of the administration of the estate. The liabilities of the administration which must be agreed and discharged include payment of the funeral account, legal and professional fees incurred during the course of the administration, reimbursement of expenses incurred by the executor, and payment of remuneration if there is an entitlement to it by virtue of a charging clause contained in the will. There may also be further tax liabilities which have accrued by reason of events occurring since the death of the deceased.

(e) To distribute to the persons entitled under the will.

In regard to (a) and (c) there is a duty to act with due diligence; by contrast, an executor has no duty to distribute to the beneficiaries before the expiration of one year from the date of death of the deceased: AEA 1925, s. 44. This period is the 'executor's year'. Even if the will directs immediate payment of a legacy, the executor cannot be compelled to pay it within the executor's year, although free to do so: see, e.g., *Pearson* v *Pearson* (1802) 1 Sch & L 10, 12. However, the legacy carries simple interest from the time for payment fixed in the will. The rate at present is 6 per cent: RSC O. 44, r. 10 (preserved in CPR, sch. 1). In any event, no beneficiary has a proprietary right to any of the assets of the estate until they are no longer required for the purposes of administration. When the executors no longer require property for the purpose of administration, it is passed by assent, which can be written, oral, or implied from conduct, except for an assent of a legal estate in land, which must be in writing: AEA 1925, s. 36(4). Compare the situation where an equitable interest in land is to be transferred: *Re Edwards' Will Trusts* [1982] Ch 30, CA.

### 6.4.3 TRANSFER TO TRUSTEES

If the will sets up continuing trusts, or if trusts arise by operation of law — as when one or more beneficiaries have not attained the age of 18 and are consequently unable to give a good discharge — a change occurs in the capacity in which the assets are held when the administration of the estate of the deceased is completed. Whether or not the executors and the trustees are the same persons, the executors should assent the property which is subject to the trusts of the will to the trustees. Although it had for many years been the practice to neglect this step where the same person ceased to hold a legal estate in one capacity and began to hold it in another, it is now settled law that it must be taken: *Re King's Will Trusts* [1964] Ch 542. Compare *King's* case with *Re Cockburn's Will Trusts* [1957] Ch 438, where it was held that personal representatives, having completed their administrative duties under the will, became trustees and could appoint new trustees of the will under the statutory power contained in the Trustee Act 1925 (TA 1925), s. 36. Any steps necessary for the effective transfer of property of a particular nature (e.g. shares) must also be taken. Once all this has been done, the trustees hold the property subject to the continuing trusts of the will. Whether administration has been completed is always a question of fact: *Re Tankard* [1942] Ch 69. There is a good deal of case law, not altogether consistent, dealing with the question of the capacity in which persons appointed as executors and trustees hold property on the occurrence of various events: *Attenborough* v *Solomon*

[1913] AC 76; *Re Ponder* [1921] 2 Ch 59; *Harvell v Foster* [1954] 1 QB 591, revsd. [1954] 2 QB 367, CA; and see *Pearson v Pearson* (1802) 1 Sch & L 10. In practice it is not always easy to tell and if in doubt it may be better to assume that executors have not become trustees.

### 6.4.4 THE BROAD STRUCTURE

Like any other legal document, a will should be set out, so far as possible, logically and chronologically. This principle demands that the testator or testatrix should begin by dating the will, and declaring that the will is his last will and that it revokes all other wills and codicils. This will greatly simplify the task of the persons who are concerned with carrying into effect the wishes expressed in the will, should there be any subsequent dispute as to which of a number of testamentary documents should be admitted to probate. Since the estate then vests in the executors, the next part of the will should be concerned with their appointment and with the duties which they have to carry out. The remainder of the dispositive part of the will then sets out the trusts on which the property not so far disposed of is to be held.

Usually it is advisable to separate the dispositive and administrative parts of the will. The administrative part follows the dispositive part, and may be contained in clauses within the body of the will, or put into a schedule. Finally, any other schedules which are to be included should appear, and the will ends with the testimonium and attestation.

For contrasting ways of setting out precedents involving administrative powers, see: *Practical Trust Precedents*, Longman, with periodic updates, and James Kessler, *Drafting Trusts and Will Trusts — A Modern Approach*, 1997, Sweet & Maxwell. An illustration of a very simple will is the following will of Matthew Stonewall.

## Will of Matthew Stonewall

THIS IS THE LAST WILL of me Matthew George Stonewall of Sodor House, Little Fitchcombe, Suffolk.

1.   I REVOKE all former wills and codicils.

2.   I appoint Felicity Stonewall of 28 Harold Hill Road, Harold Hill Essex and Xavier Benton of 69 Fitche Lane, Fitchcombe, Suffolk to be the Executors and Trustees (hereinafter called my 'Trustees') of this my Will.

3.   I give a legacy of £20,000 free of tax to the Fitchcombe Donkey Sanctuary, a registered charity. I declare that the receipt of the treasurer or other proper officer of the said Fitchcombe Donkey Sanctuary shall constitute good and valid receipt to my Trustees.

4.   I give a legacy of £10,000 to my friend Robert Smith of 28 High Street Fitchcombe. I declare that the said legacy should be paid free of tax.

5.   I give all of my estate and effects not hereby or by any codicil hereto otherwise effectively disposed of including any property over which I have a general power of disposition by will to my Trustees upon trust to sell call in and convert the same or such part thereof as shall not consist of ready moneys with full power to postpone such sale calling in and conversion without being responsible for any loss thereby occasioned and out of the net moneys that arise from such sale and any ready moneys comprised in my estate to pay my debts, testamentary and funeral expenses (including all inheritance tax and any other taxes payable on or by reason of my death in respect of property devolving under this my Will) and to invest the residue thereof (hereinafter called my Residuary Estate) in any of the investments hereby authorised.

6.   I direct that my Residuary Estate can be invested in any investments permitted by and in a manner in accordance with the provisions of the Trustee Investments Act 1961.

7.   I direct that my trustees should hold my Residuary Estate upon trust for my dear wife Grace for life and upon her death upon trust for my nieces and nephews absolutely if there be more than one in equal shares.

8.   I declare that if any of my nieces or nephews should predecease me leaving issue his her or their share of my Residuary Estate should be held on trust for his her or their respective issue absolutely if more than one in equal shares.

9.   My Trustees shall have the power to permit any trustee who is a professional to charge and be paid for all usual professional and other fees for work done by him or her or his or her firm including work which a trustee not being a professional would have done personally.

IN WITNESS whereof I have hereunto set my hand this 6th day of January 1990.

Signed by the above-named Matthew George Stonewall as his last Will in our presence and then signed by us in the presence of each other

Matthew George Stonewall

*Matthew Stonewall*

Nicholas Michaels
23 The Avenue
Fitchcombe Meadow
Suffolk

*N Michaels*

Train Driver

Adam David
76 The High Street
Fitchcombe Meadow
Suffolk

*Adam David*

Painter

### 6.4.5 TERMS AND THEIR MEANINGS

#### 6.4.5.1 Sources of trouble

A very elaborate classification of these could be made, but for present purposes it is sufficient to consider them under three heads, namely:

(a) failure to take relevant factors into account;

(b) failure to consider relevant principles of law;

(c) use of inaccurate, ambiguous or otherwise inappropriate language.

In practice (b) and (c) often have to be kept in mind together, because the use of particular words or phrases may result in the creation of problems of construction associated with rules of law which would or might not have been brought into play had the testator's intentions been accurately expressed. The law relating to perpetuities is a particularly rich source of such difficulties.

#### 6.4.5.2 Relevant factors

When drafting a will or trust, it is clearly of crucial importance to get full, clear instructions. Particular attention needs to be paid to the nature and amount of the estate involved, and possible tax liabilities. If a person wishes to exclude someone from benefiting under his will, it is permissible under English law. There is no fixed proportion of an estate which must go to a spouse or children as is the case in many civil law systems. However, the possibility of a claim under the Inheritance (Provision for Family and Dependants) Act 1975 needs to be borne in mind. If intended beneficiaries are likely to be minors, then a trust is likely to be necessary. In most circumstances, taking account of the current tax regime, accumulation and maintenance trusts (favoured trusts) are usually the most appropriate. The current rules are contained in the Inheritance Tax Act 1984, s. 71. If relevant factors were not considered when the trust or will was created, there is a great risk, not just of ill-feeling, but also litigation. Even if there is no dispute, the family and executors may feel it necessary to go to the trouble and expense of making an application to vary the provisions of a will to take account of family and tax matters which should have been considered earlier. If such an application is made within two years of the death, the new provisions are deemed for tax purposes to have arisen under the will.

#### 6.4.5.3 Relevant law

Even if a will appears to give effect to a testator's intentions, the law may defeat those intentions in one of two ways, namely:

(a) A statute may have effect unless the will expresses a contrary intention.

(b) A principle of law may operate so as to cause the gift to fail.

*Statutory considerations*

Statutes which, in particular circumstances, may affect the will in the absence of an expressed contrary intention have been enacted to deal with a variety of circumstances.

(a) *Marriage.* The general rule is that marriage automatically revokes any will made by either party before the marriage, whether or not the party intended this to occur: Wills Act 1837, s. 18; the new s. 18 as amended by the Administration of Justice Act 1982 applies to wills made after 31 December 1982. There are two exceptions to this rule; the scope of each exception depends on whether the will was made after 1982 or before 1983. For wills made after 1925, the Law of Property Act 1925, s. 177 provides that 'a will expressed to be made in contemplation of a marriage shall . . . not be revoked by the solemnisation of the marriage contemplated'. This section has been construed as meaning that marriage revokes a will unless the whole of the will, not merely certain gifts therein, was expressed to have been made in contemplation of marriage: *Re*

*Coleman* [1976] Ch 1. Under the Wills Act 1837, s. 18(3) and (4) as amended, the will, or, as the case may be, a disposition in the will, is not revoked by marriage if it appears from the will that at the time it was made, the testator or testatrix was expecting to be married to a particular person, and that he intended that the will or disposition should not be revoked by the marriage.

(b) *Death of two or more persons where it is uncertain which survived the other.*  The Law of Property Act 1925, s. 184 provides a statutory presumption that, where two or more persons have died in circumstances rendering it uncertain which of them has survived the other or others, such deaths shall be presumed to have occurred in order of seniority. This applies whether the deaths occurred in a common disaster or separately. Since the effect of the doctrine of lapse is that (subject to certain exceptions) a beneficiary who predeceases a testator cannot take under the will, the will should be drafted to take account of the results of this statutory presumption. It is worth noting that the presumption does not apply in the case of an older intestate and the intestate's younger spouse dying in circumstances rendering it uncertain which has survived the other; the presumption is that the younger did not survive the elder: AEA 1925, s. 46(3), as amended by the Intestates' Estates Act 1952. (See Sherrin and Bonehill, *Law and Practice of Intestate Succession*, Sweet & Maxwell, pp. 164–6 and 182–9, as to the usual distribution of estates by will and the effect of studies of that matter on AEA 1925 and the amendments brought about by the 1952 Act.) It was thought that the operation of s. 184 in such circumstances would not be consistent with the presumed intention of the parties, since the result would be that the next of kin of the younger spouse (in the absence of issue) would be the major beneficiaries if both spouses died intestate. It is as well, therefore, to ascertain the intention of the testator as to the destination of any gift should events fall out so as to bring the presumption into operation.

(c) *Gifts to a child or remoter descendant of the testator.*  Under the Wills Act 1837, s. 33 in its original form, if a beneficiary under a will predeceased the testator but had issue living at the testator's death, then, subject to any contrary intention expressed in the will, the gift to the beneficiary (B) did not lapse but took effect as if B had died immediately after the testator. This meant that the gift fell into B's estate, but B's issue derived no benefit from it unless they were beneficially entitled under B's will or intestacy, as the case might be. Their existence merely prevented the doctrine of lapse from operating. Section 33 as amended by the Administration of Justice Act 1982 applies if the testator dies after 31 December 1982, and has a different effect; the gift which has been saved from lapse now takes effect as a gift to B's issue *per stirpes*. Thus, if B predeceases T leaving two children C and D, and each of them predeceases B leaving children, C's and D's children will each take half between them. Alternatively, if C survives and D does not, but leaves children, C takes half and D's children take half between them. These may not necessarily be the results that T wants; in particular, in the first case, T might well prefer the grandchildren to take *per capita*. Since the provision yields to expressed contrary intention, the draftsman should ascertain the testator's wishes in the event of that contingency occurring. It is now also appropriate to ascertain the testator's intention with respect to the fate of class gifts in this contingency, since the new s. 33(2) applies to a class gift to T's children or remoter descendants.

(d) *Dissolution of the marriage between testator and beneficiary.*  The Administration of Justice Act 1982 added a new s. 18A to the Wills Act 1837; it applies where the testator dies after 31 December 1982. Its effects are that if the testator's marriage to the beneficiary is dissolved, annulled or declared void by a court, any devise or bequest to the former spouse shall lapse and any appointment of the former spouse as executor and trustee shall lapse, except in so far as a contrary intention appears by the will. The effect of this provision is that, if the former spouse is the only beneficiary, the testator has died intestate, even though there is a gift over should the spouse fail to survive the testator: *Re Sinclair* [1985] Ch 446. This case would have been decided differently if the new section had provided that, in the specified circumstances the spouse was deemed to have predeceased the testator for all purposes of the will. Section 18A(2) declares these provisions to be without prejudice to the rights of the former spouse to apply for reasonable financial provision under s. 1(1)(b) of the 1975 Act. The new section does not apply where there has been a judicial separation.

(e) *Adopted, legitimated and illegitimate children.*

(i) Adopted children. An adopted child is treated as the legitimate child of the married couple who adopted him, or, in any other case, as the legitimate child of the adopter: Adoption Act 1976, ss. 39, 42, 46, 72 and sch. 5. Subject to any contrary intention expressed in the will the principles of construction of wills set out in that Act apply to the will of a testator who dies after 31 December 1975. The rules concern dispositions by will which depend on the date of birth of a child or children.

(ii) Legitimated children. Subject to any contrary intention, a legitimated person is entitled to take any interest under the will of a testator dying after 31 December 1975, as if that person had been born legitimate: Legitimacy Act 1976, s. 5. Similar rules of construction apply to those provided by the Adoption Act 1976.

(iii) Illegitimate children. The situation is rather more complex, as there are two Acts which affect the rules of construction. The common law position was that a gift by will to children or other relations was prima facie construed as referring only to legitimate children or, as the case might be, to relationships traced wholly through legitimate connections. The rules introduced by the Family Law Reform Acts 1969 and 1987 apply, respectively, to dispositions made by a will or codicil made after 31 December 1970 but before 4 April 1988, and after 3 April 1988: Family Law Reform Act 1969, s. 15(1); Family Law Reform Act 1987, s. 19 (the later provision abolishes most of the exceptions to the earlier provision). In each case the rules apply subject to a contrary intention expressed by the will.

*Failure of gifts*

The above paragraphs were concerned with statutes which, on the occurrence of certain events, governed the devolution of the testator's estate in the absence of an expressed contrary intention. Whether these statutes shall operate if those events occur is a matter over which the testator has control, and it is for the draftsman to ensure that effect is given to the testator's wishes as to how property should be dealt with should any of those events occur. We are concerned here with failure of gifts for a variety of other reasons. Some of these causes of failure can be avoided by having regard to the relevant principles of law and using language which will ensure that the possible source of trouble is eliminated, but some problems may arise when there are events which require that an alternative destination for the property should be provided if (say) it is not to pass as on intestacy. The most important are now considered.

(a) *Attestation by beneficiary or spouse.* The first, and probably the best known, problem is brought about by the Wills Act 1837, s. 15, which deprives an attesting witness or the witness' spouse of any benefit under the will attested by the witness. Although there are exceptions to the rule, the safest course is to ensure strict adherence to it; the consequences of allowing a beneficiary to attest a will under which he benefits can be drastic for the person who allowed it to happen: *Ross* v *Caunters* [1980] Ch 297. Although the draftsman may not be in a position to ensure that this does not occur, it would be sensible to warn the testator against permitting it to happen.

(b) *Provision void as being for a purpose contrary to public policy.* The commonest such provision is one which tends to restrain marriage or encourage the termination of an existing marriage: see the many examples given in *Jarman on Wills*, 8th edn, Rothman, pp. 1528–32. There seems to be little consistency among the reported decisions on the validity of gifts made by will on condition that the donee submits to some interference with his future activities or personal rights: *Jarman*, op. cit., pp. 1451–3; the conditions relate to, *inter alia*, residence, going abroad, assuming a particular surname, entering a specified profession, marrying a person of a given religion.

(c) *Gifts void as contrary to the rule against inalienability.* The right to alienate is one of the incidents of ownership of property, and conditions which substantially defeat this right are held to be against public policy. Thus a gift will be void if it can be effected only by holding the property indefinitely and holding it or its income for a specified purpose. Some very narrow distinctions have been drawn as to whether such a gift is for the public benefit or for individual advantage: *Rickard* v *Robson* (1862) 31 Beav 262, and compare the cases cited in argument therein; *Yeap Cheah Neo* v *Ong Cheng Neo* (1875) LR 6 PC 381.

(d) *Gifts contrary to the rule against accumulations.* Most treatments of the subject of perpetuities and accumulations begin with a discussion of the rule against perpetuities. The departure from normal practice arises from the considerations discussed at **6.4.5.1**. The application of the rule against accumulations raises no questions of construction, whereas the class closing rules, which feature prominently in the law relating to perpetuities, are rules of construction.

At common law accumulations could be directed for as long as property could be made inalienable. This state of affairs ceased to exist after the Accumulations Act 1800, sometimes referred to as the 'Thellusson Act': see *Thellusson* v *Woodford* (1799) 4 Ves Jr 227, (1805) 11 Ves Jr 112. The two reports total 154 pages, the second case occupying the House of Lords on 25 June and 'several other days' in 1805. The 1800 Act and the Accumulations Act 1892 were replaced and amended by the Law of Property Act 1925, ss. 164–166. So far as the author is aware, Mr Thellusson is the only layman to have achieved immortality by having an Act of Parliament named after him. The 1925 legislation provided four possible accumulation periods, to which a further two were added by the Perpetuities and Accumulations Act 1964 (the 1964 Act), s. 13 in the case of dispositions taking effect after 15 July 1964. Since a gift into an accumulation and maintenance trust is a potentially exempt transfer for the purpose of the Inheritance Tax Act 1984 (see ss. 3A, 63, 70, 71 and 76 of that Act), it is important to ensure that any accumulation directed by will is not invalidated by failure to comply with the statutory provisions relating to the permitted periods.

The common law rule was that if an accumulation is directed for a period which exceeds the perpetuity period, the direction to accumulate is totally void: *Marshall* v *Holloway* (1820) 2 Swan 432. The common law rule applies to accumulations for the benefit of charities: see *Martin* v *Maugham* (1844) 14 Sim 230, where it was held that, although the accumulation was void, the testator had evinced an intention to devote his estate to charitable purposes, and the doctrine of cy pres was applied. The common law rule has not been affected by the 1964 Act; the 'wait and see' provisions do not apply to accumulations. If the direction is to accumulate for a period exceeding the appropriate statutory accumulation period, but not exceeding the perpetuity period, the accumulation is good to the extent of the appropriate accumulation period and only the excess is void: *Griffiths* v *Vere* (1803) 9 Ves 127; direction in a will to accumulate for the duration of a life; held, that the accumulation took effect for the statutory period of 21 years. At that time the perpetuity period had not yet been extended to a life in being and 21 years thereafter, plus any period of gestation: see *Cadell* v *Palmer* (1833) 1 Cl & F 372. The law as to permitted accumulation periods was amended by the Accumulations Act 1892, s. 1. The appropriate period for accumulations directed by will is usually either 21 years from the testator's death or the minority or respective minorities of any person or persons living or *en ventre sa mère* at the death of the testator.

(e) *Gifts void as contrary to the rule against remoteness.* One of the longest-running developments in the history of English law is that which arose out of the conflict between the desire of landowners to control land from the grave by creating remote future interests and the policy of the courts to keep in being the right of alienation. The modern rule against perpetuities is contained in the earlier sections of the 1964 Act. At common law any future interest in property was void if it could vest outside the perpetuity period, which was a life or lives in being plus 21 years and any period of gestation. In this context, 'vest' means 'vest in interest'; the interest vests if the grantee has a present right to future possession.

An interest has vested if:

(i)   the person or persons entitled are ascertained; and

(ii)  subject to any prior interest, the interest is ready to take effect in possession immediately; and

(iii) the size of the benefit is known.

The 1964 Act made two important changes. The first is the introduction of a fixed perpetuity period not exceeding 80 years: s. 1; the second is the 'wait and see' provision whereby the interest is void only where it does actually vest outside the period: s. 3. However, it is important to keep in mind that the 1964 Act has no application unless:

(i)   the instrument or disposition takes effect after 15 July 1964; and

(ii)  the disposition would have been void at common law.

Where the 1964 Act applies, the 'wait and see' provision is always to be applied first in deciding whether a disposition which would be void at common law is saved by the Act. The other saving provisions are contained in ss. 4 and 5. Section 3(5) of the 1964 Act provides a statutory definition of 'lives in being', but, if no persons exist who fall within the definition, the period is simply 21 years, unless the statutory fixed period is used. The definition complicates the drafting of instruments because each type of life in being is defined with reference to the disposition: see e.g., the examples given in Megarry and Wade, *The Law of Real Property*, 5th edn, pp. 256–8. The will draftsman would be well advised to avoid the difficulties created by the fact that X (say) may be a life in being for the purpose of one disposition in a will, Y for another, and both of them for a third. This can be done by specifying that the perpetuity period shall be 80 years (or some lesser period) from the death of the testator.

The rule that an interest does not vest if the size of the benefit is not known makes it imperative for the will draftsman to use great care if the testator wishes to make a gift to a class of persons, because questions may arise as to whether the testator intended persons falling within the definition, but who were not in existence at his death, to benefit. If specific intention is not expressed, the so-called 'class closing rules', which are rules of construction, have to be employed. Consider the following examples of gifts by will:

(i)   £x to each of the children of P

(ii)  £y to the children of Q in equal shares absolutely

(iii) £z to such of the children of R who attain 21 in equal shares absolutely.

(Note the absence of punctuation, which is never employed in wills.)

The first disposition is not a class gift in the strict sense but a series of individual gifts to members of a class. The result of such a disposition is that only the children of P who were alive at the testator's death would take: *Ringrose* v *Bramham* (1794) 2 Cox 384; *Re Bellville* [1941] Ch 414. If it was desired that children of P born after T's death should take, the addition of the words 'whenever born' would achieve that object: *Re Edmondson's Will Trusts* [1972] 1 WLR 183. This can create inconvenience for personal representatives, as they might not safely be able to distribute the estate for a very long time; for one solution see *Defflis v Goldschmidt* (1816) 1 Mer 417.

The second disposition is a class gift in the strict sense since the gift as a whole is shared between the members. Its effect would depend on whether there were any children of Q alive at the testator's death. If so, the class closes at the testator's death; if not, it never closes and all Q's children, whenever born, are entitled to take: *Viner v Francis* (1789) 2 Cox 190; *Shepherd v Ingram* (1764) Amb 448. If that disposition had read: '£y to A for life and after her death to the children of Q in equal shares absolutely', the relevant date would be the date of A's death, not that of the testator: *Ellison v Airey* (1748) 1 Ves Sen 111; *Hutcheson v Jones* (1817) 2 Madd 124, where it was said that 'the general wish of the Court is, if it can, to include all children coming *in esse* before a determinable share becomes distributable to anyone'.

The third disposition subjects each member to a contingency, that is, reaching the specified age, so the rule is that the class closes at the testator's death if there is any member of the class who has satisfied it: *Picken v Matthews* (1878) 10 ChD 264. If no member has done so at that date, the class closes as soon as one member does so: *Andrews v Partington* (1791) 3 Bro CC 401. It is immaterial whether any member of the class is in existence at the testator's death: *Re Bleckly* [1951] Ch 740. As with the second disposition, the effect of postponement of the gift to a prior interest is to make the relevant date the date when the postponement ends.

Class closing rules, being rules of construction, yield to contrary intention expressed in the will. There are also situations in which they do not apply, e.g.: 'to the children of A, namely X, Y and Z': *Bain v Lescher* (1840) 11 Sim 397; to an unlimited class of relatives: *Re Cockle's Will Trusts* [1967] Ch 690. In *Re Harker's Will Trusts* [1969] 1 WLR 1124, Goff J said that the class closing rule should not be applied unless the instrument contains an inconsistency, for instance where there is a direction that the whole class should take and another that the fund should be divided at a moment when the whole class cannot be ascertained.

The brief introduction given above is not intended to be exhaustive, either as to perpetuities generally or as to the application of the class closing rules. It should, however, convince the will draftsman of the importance of getting precise instructions from the testator or testatrix as to whom he desires to benefit and subject to what, if any, contingency, and of making sure that the intended gift does not fail for remoteness.

(f) *Lapse.* A gift fails by the operation of this doctrine when the beneficiary predeceases the testator, and its operation cannot be excluded by a declaration in the will that it is not to apply: *Browne v Hope* (1872) LR 14 Eq 343. A substitutional gift is effective to prevent the operation of the doctrine by directing the gift elsewhere. As we have seen, statute provides for this in certain circumstances, subject to expressed contrary intention: Wills Act 1837, s. 33 (gift to testator's child or remoter descendant); see also s. 32 (entailed property). A gift to beneficiaries as joint tenants does not lapse unless they all predecease the testator. But if there are words of severance (e.g. 'to P, Q and R equally' or 'share and share alike'), or if the gift is made to them as tenants in common, the gift of the share of any beneficiary who predeceases the testator fails. If a gift, on the true construction of the words, is a class gift to persons who are to be ascertained from some general description, the doctrine does not apply.

(g) *Ademption.* Legacies may be specific, general or demonstrative. Devises may be specific or general. Of these, only specific legacies and devises are subject to the doctrine of ademption. The two characteristics of a specific legacy (or devise) are that it must be a part of the testator's personal (or real) property and must be specified so as to be separated or distinguished from the general mass of his estate. A specific gift of either nature fails by ademption if its subject matter has ceased to exist as part of the testator's estate at death. If the subject matter of the gift is sold or converted into some other form of personal property, the beneficiary is not, unless the will so provides, entitled to receive the traceable proceeds of sale or the property into which the gift has been converted: *Re Lewis' Will Trusts* [1937] Ch 118 (bequest of certain securities 'or the investments representing the same at my death if they shall have been converted into other holdings'; one of the securities redeemed and the money placed on deposit; held, the money on deposit was an investment representing the security and the gift was not adeemed). A frequent (and disastrous) example of ademption is where the testator leaves his home to a beneficiary, carefully describing it by its address and then moves house. This can be avoided by a more generalised description, e.g., 'the house in which I shall be living at the date of my death'. Note that the doctrine does not apply if the existence of the property is to be ascertained as at the date of death, whether expressly or by the operation of the Wills Act 1837, s. 24(1). If T bequeaths to A 'the Rolls-Royce motor car which I own at my death' or 'my Rolls-Royce motor car' without reference to a time at which it was owned, and T owns no Rolls-Royce motor car at the date of death, the gift is not adeemed; as referred to, it never existed as part of T's estate.

Subject to contrary intention, the effect of failure, whether by lapse or (in the case of a specific gift) ademption is that a legacy or a specific devise which fails falls into residue, or if there is no residuary gift, goes as on intestacy. As to specific gifts, see *Wainman* v *Field* (1854) Kay 507: a gift of leasehold property declared to be exonerated from payments of debts and legacies was bad for remoteness; held, because of the exoneration, it did not fall into residue but passed to the next of kin. As to residue, see *Vaudrey* v *Howard* (1853) 2 WR 32: gift of six-sevenths of residue to six persons, but in certain events two of them were not to take; the events occurred; held, the remaining four took the entire six-sevenths between them. A residuary gift which fails goes as on intestacy.

# 6.5 Inaccurate or Ambiguous Terms

## 6.5.1 EQUIVOCAL DESCRIPTIONS

If it is not possible to identify either the subject matter or the object of a gift after taking into account any admissible extrinsic evidence and applying any relevant rules of construction, the gift will fail. Where the testator has died after 31 December 1982, the admissibility of extrinsic evidence in the interpretation of the will is governed by the Administration of Justice Act 1982, s. 21. The task of the will draftsman in this respect is to ensure that there is no need to resort to extrinsic evidence. Equivocal descriptions are therefore to be avoided; make sure that there is a description. The following cases illustrate this point. In *Hunt* v *Hort* (1791) 3 Bro CC 311 the legacy to Lady (blank space) was void 'as not being named in the will'. Compare this with *Price* v *Page* (1799) 4 Ves Jr 680, where the legacy to (blank) Price was good, there being positive evidence that the claimant was the person whom the testator intended to benefit. In *Asten* v *Asten* [1894] 3 Ch 260, there were separate gifts to each of four sons of 'All that newly built house being no. (blank space) Sudeley Place'; the testator owned four such houses. The gift failed for uncertainty. Other problems arise where there has been a failure to check the family circumstances and there is more than one beneficiary answering to the description: *Re Jackson* [1933] Ch 237 (three nephews all named Arthur Murphy).

## 6.5.2 PRESUMPTIONS IN CONSTRUCTION

Presumptions exist for the determination of the meaning of the language used in a will. This is a topic which has been very extensively treated in various books: *Jarman on Wills*, op. cit.; Williams, Mortimer and Sunnucks, *Executors, Administrators and Probate*; Hawkins and Ryder, *The Construction of Wills*, 3rd edn, 1938, Sweet & Maxwell; Theobald, *The Law of Wills*, 15th edn, Sweet & Maxwell.

The first of the two basic presumptions is that, prima facie, words are to be given their ordinary meaning. This is rebuttable by showing that the testator used the word in a different sense from its ordinary meaning in one of the following two ways:

(a) There is a secondary meaning which makes sense in the context when the normal meaning does not, as in the shortest will ever to be admitted to probate, consisting of the three words 'all for mother', by which last word the testator was understood to mean his wife: *Thorn* v *Dickens* [1906] WN 54.

(b) By the application of the so-called 'dictionary' principle, whereby the testator has made it clear in the will that the word is being used in a sense different from its accepted sense — 'Testators can make 'black' mean 'white' if they make the dictionary sufficiently clear': *Re Cook* [1948] Ch 212, per Harman J.

The second presumption is that technical words are to be given their technical meaning; this can be rebutted in the same two ways as can the first presumption.

It would be impossible, in a treatment as short as this, to deal in any detail with the many problems of construction involving frequently used words and phrases. The index to *Jarman* contains 10 pages of entries referring to the construction of words. There is no easy solution for the will draftsman who has to ascertain whether the word or phrase, the use of which is contemplated, is apt to produce the desired effect. One word, however, deserves special mention; it is the word 'money'. *Jarman* (op. cit., pp. 1009–14) cites over 50 cases. See, especially, the comment at p. 1011 referring to *Perrin* v *Morgan* [1943] AC 399: 'the House of Lords decision evoked expressions of public approval and humorous comment not usually associated with decisions on the interpretation of wills'. The words used in *The Times* (26 January 1943, fourth leader) about the decision in *Perrin* v *Morgan* on the interpretation of that word form a fitting conclusion to this section:

'The question is', said Alice, 'whether you can make words mean so many different things.'

'The question is', said Humpty Dumpty, 'which is to be Master — that's all.'

# 6.6     Trustees' Powers and Duties

## 6.6.1    APPROACHING PROBLEMS INVOLVING TRUSTEES' POWERS AND DUTIES

### 6.6.1.1    A general guide
These notes give broad guidance on the situations in which you may be asked to give advice involving the extent of trustees' powers and duties. This is in no way a comprehensive guide, just a broad summary to give a starting point.

Clear and accurate analysis is one of the most vital skills in trust cases. Each aspect of the case must be clarified and kept clear in the mind, using a high standard of fact management skills. The following areas may require attention:

(a) Timing. Are you being asked to advise on setting up a trust, or on problems with an existing trust?

(b) The role of people. Who are the trustees? Who are the beneficiaries? Precisely what interest does each beneficiary have?

(c) The assets in the trust. What constitutes the capital of the trust? What income is produced?

(d) The issues. What precisely is in issue in the case? Is it something that has been done or that may be done? Who has been or may be affected?

In advising on the powers and duties of trustees, there are three broad categories:

(a) Those which are mandatory by statute and may not be avoided. You must be aware of these, and explain them properly to a client when appropriate.

(b) Those which are implied by statute, but which may be excluded. You must consider whether these are or should be expressly or impliedly excluded.

(c) Those which are specifically inserted by the settlor in a particular trust. As appropriate, the terms to be included, or the meaning of the specific terms which have been included, must be properly considered.

### 6.6.1.2 Drafting a trust document

In drawing up a trust document, whether *inter vivos* or in a will, the full range of powers and duties to be given to the trustees must be carefully and individually considered, and discussed with the settlor. Those terms which apply automatically by statute must be explained. Those terms which will apply unless they are excluded must be considered to see whether they should be excluded. Then consider what extra terms should be included.

It is important to ensure that the terms do exactly achieve what the settlor wishes to achieve, that they are comprehensive, and that they are absolutely accurate and unambiguous. You must look to the future as far as possible, and try to cover all foreseeable eventualities.

Many trusts will be drawn up by solicitors, often on the basis of standard-form precedents. You will normally only be approached for advice if there is some special complexity in the facts, or in the drafting requirements of a particular clause.

### 6.6.1.3 Scope of powers

Once a trust has been set up, questions may arise as to what can properly be done within its terms. The question may arise because the trustees are unsure whether they have the power to carry out a particular transaction. Alternatively, a beneficiary may wish the trustees to take a particular course of action which they are unsure about or unwilling to take.

Sometimes a court action may be required to settle the matter. There are three basic possibilities:

### 6.6.1.4 A construction application

This is generally commenced by a Part 8 application under the Civil Procedure Rules 1998, asking the court to construe and interpret powers and duties in a trust where the position is not clear.

The application should be brought by the trustees if there is any genuine concern about the meaning or application of any provision. All parties who may have an interest in the outcome should be made parties or someone from a class of beneficiaries should be made a party with a representation order to represent the others with the same interest.

Care should be taken to include those who stand to gain if the provision is held to be invalid. In particular the residuary legatees if the problem is to do with the validity of a legacy, the persons entitled under an intestacy if the problem concerns a gift of the residuary estate under a will, the settlor or those entitled under the will or upon intestacy of the settlor if the problem concerns a provision in an *inter vivos* settlement need to be parties. Also if a charitable bequest is involved the Attorney-General needs to be joined, as one of the options will be that the gift should be applied cy près.

An example of a construction problem and a possible draft is given here to illustrate the process.

RE ALBURY'S WILL

---

INSTRUCTIONS TO COUNSEL
TO DRAFT PROCEEDINGS

---

£375

Redman and Jackson
1 First Avenue Lane
Angmering
East Sussex

INSTRUCTIONS TO COUNSEL

Counsel has herewith:

(1)   Copy of Will of Albert Albury

(2)   Statement of Steven Palmer

(3)   Letter from Adam Nicholas

Instructing Solicitors act for Miss Emily Palmer and Mr Gary Palmer, the executors and trustees of their late uncle, Mr Albert Albury's will.

Mr Albury died in October 1998. Probate was granted of a will dated 6 September 1998 to Miss and Mr Palmer on 10 January 1999.

Mr Albury had been a client of this firm for many years, as have the Palmers. Instructing Solicitors did have in our safe keeping a will written by Mr Albury in 1985 leaving all his estate to his children. However, after his death a will dated 6 September 1998 was found in his room at the Abbeyfield Nursing Home in Rustington, East Sussex, where he spent the last two months of his life.

A copy of this will is enclosed with these Instructions. It appears to be authentic and in a valid form although unfortunately Mr Albury does not appear to have taken any professional advice on the drafting of the document.

Two of Mr Albury's children, Edward and Helen Albury have expressed disquiet about this will. Mr and Miss Palmer are concerned that after some preliminary investigations there do appear to be some difficulties in interpreting the will and wish to resolve any problems in as swift and easy a manner as possible to avoid family wranglings.

It should perhaps be added that Mr and Miss Palmer both visited their uncle frequently while he was at the Nursing Home and although he was clearly gravely ill and often in pain, they both confirm that he appeared lucid and mentally alert.

As Counsel can see the will contains several pecuniary legacies. No difficulties arise with the legacy to Mr Khan. However, having made enquiries, it appears that there is no registered charity of the name 'the Sussex Hospice Movement'. Instructing Solicitors have taken a statement from Mr Steven Palmer, Gary Palmer's 19-year-old son which appears to shed some light on what Mr Albury meant.

The Trustees have contacted the East Sussex Home for the Incurably Ill. It is a registered charity running several homes in Sussex. They are willing (indeed, perhaps not surprisingly, keen) to accept the legacy if Mr Albury did mean them to receive it.

The third legacy causes the executors great concern. They, and the family, are happy that Mr Albury wished to benefit the Home where all considered he was well looked after but the executors are unsure who should benefit and whether the money should be divided up or used for a single purchase as suggested in Mr Nicholas, the manager of the Home's letter.

The remaining pecuniary legacy 'to each and every spouse of any and each of my children and grandchildren' is rather unfortunate. Mr Albury had four children. Helen is unmarried. Mr Albury's eldest son died tragically a few days before his father. As Mr Albury was so ill the news was kept from him. Philip left a widow Georgina and a daughter who is unmarried. The second son Matthew has not been seen by the rest of the family for some time. He is believed to be in the South of France. His wife Sophia lives in Brighton with their son Jean-Pierre and his wife, Marina. Edward, the youngest, lives in Lewes with Juliette Jones. Edward and Juliette have been together for 20 years but the executors understand that they have never got round to marrying. The executors are concerned that Edward will be very aggrieved if Juliette is excluded, particularly as Jean-Pierre and Marina have only been married a year. The trustees inform Instructing Solicitors that Mr Albury was on good terms with Edward and Juliette but probably did not know they were not married.

The executors are keen to discuss the situation with Mr Albury's children as soon as possible. Accordingly, Counsel is instructed to draft a construction claim to seek the determination of the court on any issue Counsel considers is appropriate. An Opinion will be of great assistance in due course but counsel is instructed to draft proceedings first.

THIS IS THE LAST WILL of me Albert ALBURY currently residing at Abbeyfield Nursing Home Rustington in the County of East Sussex

1.  I REVOKE all former Wills and Codicils

2.  I appoint Mr Gary Palmer of Blue Cottage Redpath Lane Rustington and Miss Emily Palmer of 222 Brighton Road Brighton to be the Executors and Trustees of this my Will (hereinafter called 'My Trustees')

3.  I give a legacy of £500 to my friend Mr M Khan of 6 Softon Road Rustington

4.  I give a legacy of £1,000 to the Sussex Hospice Movement

5.  I give a legacy of £9,000 to the nurses at the Abbeyfield Nursing Home with my deep gratitude

6.  I give a legacy of £2,000 each to each and every spouse of my children and grandchildren

7.  I devise and give all my real and personal property not hereby disposed of to my Trustees upon trust to sell the same with power to postpone the sale to pay my just debts, funeral expenses, tax payable on my death and the aforementioned legacies and then to pay and apply the residue to my children and if more than one in equal shares

8.  If any of my children should die before me I direct that their share be taken by any child or children of that child and if more than one in equal shares

Signed by Albert Albury on 6 September 1998 in the presence of the witnesses who have signed below in my presence and in the presence of each other

Albert Albury

*Albert Abury*

Witnessed by Emeline Bentley
62 Cave End Road
Bognor Regis

*E Bentley*

Housewife

George Martin
8 Grove Road
Angmering

*George Martin*

Doctor

STATEMENT OF STEVEN PALMER

I am a great-nephew of the late Albert Albury. I am 19 years old. I work as a sales assistant in Boots in Angmering. I was very fond of my great-uncle and when I heard he was ill I tried to visit him when I got the chance. One day I was unexpectedly given the afternoon off. I believe this was 3rd September last year. I went to see Great-Uncle Albert. He was on his own in his room looking at the local newspaper. He showed me an article about a hospice in the area which was short of funds. They were appealing for money to improve the buildings and grounds. I did not look at the article in great detail but I believe the name of the Home was the East Sussex Home for the Incurably Ill. He was rather upset about the article and said to me that he was going to try and help by leaving them some money in his will. He said not to tell the rest of the family because he did not want to be bothered with lots of suggestions for alternative good causes.

*Abbeyfield Nursing Home*
*Rustington*
*East Sussex*
*BN5 3HU*

28 February 1999

Dear Mr and Miss Palmer

**RE: Mr A Albury deceased**

Thank you for your letter of 7 February. There is nothing in the contracts of staff at the home to prohibit them receiving money in a will of a late patient as long as the family is happy. Currently we have 18 qualified nurses working full-time at the home and 6 part-time. 2 of the full-timers have joined this month. One person who was here in Mr Albury's time with us has left. We also employ 6 nursing assistants and 3 student nurses. It would be possible to find out who worked on the Abbeyside wing where Mr Albury was but it would be administratively time consuming. If it was possible I would suggest the money could be used for a single purchase such as an improvement to staff facilities which all the staff would benefit from. Let me know how things progress.

With best regards
Yours sincerely

Adam Nicholas
Manager

Details to be filled in on Claim Form N208

IN THE HIGH COURT OF JUSTICE                                    Claim No.
CHANCERY DIVISION

BETWEEN

(1)  EMILY PALMER
(2)  GARY PALMER                                               Claimants

and

(1)  THE EAST SUSSEX HOME FOR THE INCURABLY ILL
(2)  [A NURSE]
(3)  THE ABBEYFIELD NURSING HOME
(4)  GEORGINA ALBURY
(5)  JULIETTE [      ]
[(6)  SOPHIA ALBURY]
(7)  HELEN ALBURY
(8)  MATTHEW ALBURY
(9)  EDWARD ALBURY
(10)  [PHILIP'S DAUGHTER]
(11)  HER MAJESTY'S ATTORNEY-GENERAL              Defendants

_____

CLAIM FORM (CPR PART 8)
_____

The Claimants seek the determination of the court on the following issues arising out of the construction of the Will of Albert Albury dated 6th September 1998. The Claimants are the executors and trustees named in the will and probate was granted to them on 10 January 1999.

The questions which the Claimants seek determination of the court on and the following remedies are:

1.    That it may be decided whether on the true construction of the said will and in the events which have happened the legacy to the Sussex Hospice Movement is:

(a)   a valid gift to the East Sussex Home for the Incurably Ill, a registered charity; or

(b)   is an effective gift to any other and if so which institution trust or corporation;

(c)   is not an effective gift to any specific institution trust or corporation.

2.    If the answer to the question in paragraph 1 is in sense (c) that it may be determined whether upon the true construction of the will and in the events which have happened the said legacy is:

(a)   a gift for general charitable purposes and is applicable cy près; or

(b)   is undisposed by the will and falls into the residue.

3.    If the answer to the question in paragraph 2 is in sense (a) that the Court may direct a scheme for the application of the said legacy.

4.    That it may be determined on the true construction of the will and in the events which have happened whether any or all of the following are entitled to legacies under clause 6 of the will as 'spouses' of any of the testator's children:

(a)   the fourth defendant [who is a widow];

(b) the fifth defendant [who has lived with a son of the testator for many years but is not married to him];

[(c) the sixth defendant [who is married to       ?] but separated from a son of the testator].

5.   That it may be determined on the true construction of the will and in the events which have happened whether the legacy under clause 5 of the will is:

(a) a valid gift to the 3rd Defendants;

(b) a valid gift to be divided between a class of nurses at the Abbeyfield Nursing Home;

(c) is void for uncertainty or otherwise.

6.   If the answer to the question in paragraph 5 is in sense (b) that it may be determined on the true construction of the will and in the events which have happened whether the clause includes:

(a) only qualified nurses or extends to nursing assistants and or student nurses;

(b) only staff working on the Abbeyside wing or extends to staff in the whole hospital;

(c) only staff who were working at the hospital at the time Mr Albury was there and are still there or extends to those who have left since and or those who have joined since.

7.   The second defendant may be appointed to represent any nurses or other staff at the Abbeyfield Nursing Home who claim to be beneficially entitled to a share of the legacy under clause 5 of the will.

8.   That provision may be made for the costs of this application.

9.   Further or other relief.

10. The claim is made under RSC O. 85, r. 2 as preserved by CPR, sch. 1.

STATEMENT OF TRUTH

The Claimants believe that the facts stated in the Particulars of Claim are true. I am duly authorised by the Claimant to sign this statement.

Full Name Emily Palmer and Gary Palmer

Name of Claimants' solicitors     Redman and Jackson,
                                  1 First Avenue Lane
                                  Angmering
                                  East Sussex

Signed June Johnson               partner

Dated etc.

**6.6.1.5    An application under the Trustee Act 1925, s. 57**
An application to the court for approval of a particular transaction that cannot be carried out under the existing powers and duties of the trustees. Such an application can be made under the Trustee Act (TA) 1925, s. 57.

Section 57 provides:

*(1)   Where in the management or administration of any property vested in trustees, any sale, lease, mortgage, surrender, release, or other disposition, or any purchase, investment, acquisition, expenditure or other transaction, is in the opinion of the court expedient, but the same cannot be effected by reason of the absence of any power for that purpose vested in the trustees by the trust instrument, if any, or by law, the court may by order confer upon the trustees, either generally or in any particular instance, the necessary power for the purpose, on such terms, and subject to such provisions and conditions, if any, as the court may think fit and may direct in what manner any money authorised to be expended, and the costs of any transaction, are to be paid or borne as between capital and income.*

*(2)   The court may, from time to time, rescind or vary any order made under this section, or may make any new or further order.*

*(3)   An application to the court under this section may be made by the trustees, or by any of them, or by any person beneficially interested under the trust.*

*(4)   This section does not apply to trustees of a settlement for the purposes of the Settled Land Act 1925.*

### 6.6.1.6   A variation of trust claim

This may be brought where the existing terms of the trust are not adequate to achieve a particular purpose. An application can be made to alter administrative or dispositive powers. Where the beneficaries are of full age and all are ascertained, the consent of all the beneficiaries should be obtained for any proposed change and there is then no need to go to court. If all the beneficiaries cannot agree then the change cannot be made. The Variation of Trusts Act 1958 allows the court to give consent to a change to provisions of a trust on behalf of beneficiaries who are unable to give consent themselves, e.g., minors, those under an incapacity, those who are not yet born or otherwise ascertained. Before an application can be made any beneficiaries who do exist and are of full age and capacity must consent to the proposal, otherwise the application cannot be heard. The court will grant the application if it considers it in the best interests of the people on whose behalf it is being asked to grant consent.

The 1958 Act does not apply to charitable trusts as there are no beneficiaries upon whose behalf the court could be asked to grant consent.

### 6.6.1.7   Breaches of powers and duties

A beneficiary may seek your advice where it is alleged that there is a breach of any power or duty. This may involve considering what powers and duties there are expressly or impliedly in the trust, whether there has in fact been any breach of any such duty, if so who is liable for the breach, and what the appropriate measure for assessing liability is.

If there has in fact been a breach, you must:

(a)   identify each breach separately as each is a separate cause of action;

(b)   identify the precise facts of each breach, including dates, what precisely was done, what power or duty was breached and how, etc.;

(c)   identify who to allege to be liable for each breach.

To establish who may be liable:

(a)   Decide whether all the trustees will be sued as being jointly and severally liable. Normally one trustee will be held liable for the acts of another due to joint and several liability, either because they have acquiesced in an action, or because they have failed to monitor properly what a co-trustee is doing. There are exceptions — where, for example, a non-qualified trustee defers to the advice of a legally qualified trustee: *Head* v *Gould* [1898] 2 Ch 250. Note that a professional trustee may be seen as having a higher level of duty than a non-professional trustee: *Bartlett* v *Barclays Bank Trust Co. Ltd (No. 1)* [1980] Ch 515. Also consider whether any trustee may have a defence under TA 1925, s. 61 on the basis that he acted reasonably and ought to be excused.

(b) If an agent is involved, decide whether the agent can be sued personally, and if so on what basis. Also decide whether the trustees are or are not likely to be held liable for the acts of the agent (see TA 1925, ss. 23 and 30).

(c) Decide if, on the facts, one of the beneficiaries is involved in the breach, and if so whether TA 1925, s. 62 may be invoked.

(d) Consider the effect of any clause purporting to exempt the trustees from liability: *Armitage* v *Nurse* [1997] 2 All ER 705 and *Wight* v *Olswang* (1999) *The Times*, 18 May 1999, CA.

As regards remedies, it is important to decide what may be recovered for the breach:

(a) Money. Consider the measure of liability for each trustee. Will the trustee be able to pay if found liable? Consider separately loss of capital and loss of income. Note that, strictly speaking, the remedy for a beach of trust is not damages but an account.

(b) Trust property. This may be recovered by tracing, or by a constructive trust. Is an item of particular importance to the beneficiary? Is tracing particularly useful as the trustee may not be able to pay all he is found liable to pay? For tracing against innocent parties, see *Foskett* v *McKeown* [1997] 3 All ER 392.

(c) The range of remedies. Declarations may be made, enquiries, etc., may be ordered. Note that vesting orders for property may be required: TA 1925, ss. 44–56.

It is vital to keep practical points in mind:

(a) Remember that many trusts involve different members of the same family. In advising an action against a trustee or a beneficiary one may be advising the client to sue a close relative.

(b) If you are suing a trustee, do you wish to replace him, or to ask the court to replace him: TA 1925, ss. 36 and 41?

(c) It may be possible to avoid going to court in some circumstances, if all the potential beneficiaries are adults and of full capacity and they all agree to a particular transaction: *Saunders* v *Vautier* (1841) Cr & Ph 240. Under the Trusts of Land and Appointment of Trustees Act 1996 where there is no one appointed by the trust instrument and the beneficiaries fulfil the *Saunders* v *Vautier* criteria they may give written directions to trustees to retire or appoint new trustees subject to certain conditions without going to court: ss. 19 and 20.

(d) The costs of the action will normally be paid from the trust fund (though trustees guilty of misconduct will pay the court personally). Long legal arguments may thus cut down what the client recovers.

An example of a basic breach of trust problem and a possible draft follows.

Re BABBLE'S TRUST

## INSTRUCTIONS TO COUNSEL TO ADVISE

Minifirm and Partners
64 Pantiles
Chichester
West Sussex

## INSTRUCTIONS TO COUNSEL

Mr Mark Fairbrother, a long-standing commercial client of ours, has approached the writer of these instructions with queries over the running of a trust set up by his late wife's father. Mr Fairbrother's children, Chloe and Adam, are beneficiaries. Chloe has just celebrated her 18th birthday and Adam is 20.

We have not been able to obtain a copy of the trust deed but have been able to get a reasonably clear idea of the terms from our clients. Mr Joseph Babble set up the trust on 9 May 1990. He appointed his two daughters Mrs Jane Fairbrother and Mrs Suzanne Babble-Clark as trustees along with a long-standing friend of Mr Babble, a Mr Martin Nickelby. Sadly Mr Babble died in 1992 and Mrs Fairbrother the following year. The remaining trustees declined to appoint a new trustee.

The beneficiaries are Adam and Chloe and their cousins, Mrs Babble-Clark's sons, Benjamin who is 17, and Xavier who is 22 years old. We understand that there is a standard accumulation and maintenance trust with the grandchildren receiving income once they reach 19 and capital at 25. There is a power to apply income during a beneficiary's minority for his or her education or other benefit and a power to advance up to a half of the grandchild's prospective share of the capital. The capital in the trust fund is currently about £80,000.

Chloe and Adam's school fees were paid by the trust. Adam now receives a quarterly cheque and Chloe has had half her college fees paid. The Fairbrothers are happy with these arrangements; however, certain other aspects give them great cause for concern.

Mr Fairbrother who is a financial director of a large ceramics factory has made some enquiries about how the trust funds are invested. In May 1994 the trustees bought a sailing boat which cost £6,000. When questioned about this Mrs Babble-Clark apparently told our clients it was an excellent investment for the future. Xavier is apparently a keen sailor. Adam and Chloe have been invited to use the boat but Mr Fairbrother, quite rightly in our view, feels that this was not a proper use of the investment powers and if Xavier wanted a boat it should have been bought with his share.

Even more worrying is the trustees' decision last month to loan £20,000 from the trust funds to Mr Joseph Babble's brother, Harold. Mr Fairbrother has only just discovered this transaction as a result of information from Harold's estranged wife Clara. Harold Babble runs various businesses, including a video distribution warehouse where Mrs Babble-Clark and her husband work. Mr Fairbrother informs us Harold Babble is a charming plausible man who, while probably not involved in anything very criminal, 'sails close to the wind'. His businesses were in some financial trouble and, according to Clara Babble, her husband was being pursued by a very unsavoury character who threatened to break his legs if he did not pay £10,000 which he owed. Mrs Babble-Clark convinced the other trustee that it was not in the grandchildren's best interest to have their great-uncle involved in such matters or to have him go bankrupt and Mrs Babble-Clark and her husband lose their jobs.

Mrs Babble has told our clients that the remaining £10,000 was paid by her husband to Harold Babble Enterprises Limited, allegedly to pay back a loan Harold made himself from the company. He then ordered Mrs Babble as the only other director of the company to join him in authorising the transfer of the money to another company, Harold Babble Enterprises Limited. The money is, as far as she knows, still in the company's bank account at the Chester Branch of National Westminster.

Mr Fairbrother believes that some of the rest of the trust funds is invested in Mr Harold Babble's companies and is therefore at risk.

Instructing Solicitors have raised these grave concerns with the trustees but they do not appear to appreciate the seriousness of the situation. We feel that it is necessary, if Counsel advises there are good grounds, to institute breach of trust proceedings against the trustees. Our clients would also like to apply to have the trustees replaced.

Counsel is instructed to draft appropriate proceedings. It is appreciated that Counsel does not have all the information which ideally we would have liked to provide but it is felt that the situation is urgent and it is necessary to institute proceedings now to try to prevent further harm.

Counsel is not asked to provide a full opinion on the strengths of the case at this stage, although a note of any particularly important points on the draft proceedings would of course be very helpful. Counsel is asked to provide a short opinion on two points. If our clients are unable to recover against the trustees, they would like to know whether they can proceed against Mr Harold Babble, and if so, what would this involve and what are their prospects of success? Mr Fairbrother has heard that beneficiaries have acquired new rights and he wishes to know whether these would help in this situation.

Counsel is so instructed to advise.

Razor Cottage
68 Sharp Street
Isleworth
Middlesex

2 March 1999

Dear Chloe and Adam

I was rather surprised at your letter. At your age you should not be worrying about financial details, you should be getting on with your studies and enjoying yourselves. I do understand that the questions were not of your making.

There is nothing that need concern you. You have always received generous support and will receive a handsome sum when you are old enough to deal with your own finances.

I am sorry but I am not prepared to go to the trouble of copying all the documents and explaining them to you. It is really not necessary. All is under control. I am surprised you do not wish to help out your great-uncle. I believe it is in children's best interests that families stick together. I am sure you would both agree when you think about it. There is more than enough in the fund for your needs.

Birthday greetings to Chloe.

With best wishes

*Martin Nickelby*

Martin Nickelby

Razor Cottage
68 Sharp Street
Isleworth
Middlesex

21 March 1999

Dear Sir

**Re BABBLE TRUST**

Mrs Babble-Clark and I were amazed at your recent letter. This is all a fuss about nothing. The children are sweet sensible kids who are perfectly happy with the provision made for them by their grandfather. It is a pity that you and they are being used by their father to pursue perceived grievances of his own.

Mr Babble trusted our business sense and integrity. We were given absolute discretion. The trust deed says specifically that we should treat the money as if we owned it ourselves when we choose investments. It would be wrong for us to take account of the views of some of the beneficiaries or rather the father of them. Accordingly we are unable to comply with your requests for information as we would be failing in our duties.

Yours faithfully

*Martin Nickelby*

Martin Nickelby

IN THE HIGH COURT OF JUSTICE
CHANCERY DIVISION

BETWEEN

(1)   ADAM FAIRBROTHER
(2)   CHLOE FAIRBROTHER

Claimants

and

(1)   SUZANNE BABBLE-CLARK
(2)   MARTIN NICKLEBY

Defendants

PARTICULARS OF CLAIM

1.   By a settlement dated 9 May 1990 ('the settlement') made between (1) Joseph Babble ('the settlor') and (2) Jane Fairbrother and the Defendants, the Settlor appointed Jane Fairbrother and the Defendants to be trustees of the settlement and vested in them the property set out in the schedule to the Settlement ('the trust property'). [The trustees were given absolute discretion subject to their fiduciary duties to invest the trust property in any investments as if they were the beneficial owners.]

2.   The Defendants are the surviving trustees of the Settlement, Jane Fairbrother having died in [date]. The Claimants are beneficiaries under the Settlement.

3.   In or around May 1994 the Defendants purchased purportedly as an investment a sailing boat using trust funds.

4.   In or around May 1996 the Defendants loaned £20,000 from the trust funds to Harold Babble who is not a beneficiary under the Settlement.

[5.   At various times varying amounts of trust property have been and remain invested in companies run, owned or otherwise controlled by the said Harold Babble despite concerns over the financial state of the companies.]

6.   The Defendants are in breach of their obligations as trustees by purchasing the sailing boat, and/or loaning the £20,000 [and/or allowing trust funds to remain invested in the companies].

PARTICULARS OF BREACH OF TRUST

(a)   The Defendants failed to consider other more suitable investments.

(b)   The Defendants failed to take appropriate skilled advice.

(c)   The Defendants failed to maintain a proper range of investments in pursuance of their duty to diversify investments.

(d)   The sailing boat which is a wasting asset should not have been bought in purported exercise of the Defendants' investment powers.

(e)   The loan was not a proper use of the power of investment in particular no or inadequate security, no interest and no or inadequate arrangements for repayment were made.

(f)   The Defendants failed to keep the investments of the trust property under review and in particular failed to take account of the financial difficulties of companies in which the trust property had been and is invested and failed to take steps to protect the trust property.

(g) The Defendants failed to exercise their discretionary powers properly in that they took account of irrelevant or improper considerations namely the wishes and or benefit of some of the beneficiaries and or other individuals not beneficiaries under the Settlement.

AND the Claimants claim

(1) An inquiry into whether the trust property has been properly invested by the Defendants.

(2) An account of the Defendants' investments and dealings with the trust property on the footing of wilful default.

(3) Repayment of the amount found due to the trust by the inquiry and upon the account, together with interest thereon.

(4) An order that the Defendants be removed as trustees and some fit and proper person or persons be appointed to act as trustees in substitution of the Defendants or in addition to the Defendants.

(5) Such other accounts, directions and inquiries as may be necessary.

(6) Further or other relief.

(7) Costs.

STATEMENT OF TRUTH

The Claimants believe that the facts stated in these Particulars of Claim are true. I am duly authorised by the Claimants to sign this statement.

Full name
Name of Claimants' solicitors firm
Signed
Position

A BARRISTER

NOTE

RE BABBLE

1.   This note accompanies a draft Particulars of Claim for breach of trust in relation to a settlement made by Joseph Babble.

2.   I agree with Instructing Solicitors that it does appear that there is a good case against the trustees. Of course, there is not much information at present and the situation will need to be reviewed in the light of any Defence put in by the trustees and any new information.

3.   I have drafted the proceedings with both Chloe and Adam as the Claimants. Would Instructing Solicitors please confirm whether they are acting for both and whether both are happy with the proposed proceedings. As long as one beneficiary is prepared to bring the proceedings the claim can be commenced. It is not necessary to involve all the beneficiaries.

4.   The beneficiaries are entitled to see the trust deed and accounts. I have not included a demand for these in the Particulars of Claim as they will be needed earlier than the resolution of the case. A formal letter should be sent demanding the documents.

5.   I have included a request for the removal of the trustees or alternatively, additional trustees as the courts are usually reluctant to replace or supplement trustees without evidence of breaches of trust or serious incompetence. However, if it is thought that there is a substantial risk of damage to the trust funds from the present trustees continuing in office in the meantime then a Part 8 claim can be issued quickly to deal with that issue before the main claim is heard. Names can be suggested if the beneficiaries wish to put forward one or more person although there is no guarantee the court will accept their suggestions.

6.   It is possible on the information available at present that Harold Babble could be considered to be a constructive trustee of the £20,000. As he does not appear to have any of the £20,000 left in his possession the only remedy against him is a personal claim. It would be worth enquiring further as to Mr Babble's financial standing. If he is already insolvent there will be no point in issuing proceedings against him. If on the other hand it appears he has money at the moment but may not have for long it may well be worth issuing proceedings reasonably speedily if Adam and or Chloe Fairbrother wish to.

7.   If Harold Babble could show that the loan was a proper commercial transaction then he will have a complete defence to a claim for repayment to the trust fund of the money. Could Instructing Solicitors find out as much information as possible about whether there were any interest payments, arrangements for security etc.

8.   Assuming that the evidence shows that the transfer of £20,000 was more a favour than a loan it will be necessary for the beneficiaries to show 'knowing receipt'. The precise standard of knowledge required to establish a constructive trust is still not entirely clear from the case law but the beneficiaries will have to show knowledge of both the fact that the £20,000 came from trust funds and that it was an improper use of the funds. As Harold Babble actually received trust property it is likely to be enough to show that he either actually knew these facts or 'shut his eyes to the obvious' and 'wilfully or recklessly' failed to make 'such enquiries as a reasonable and honest man would make' (*Re Montagu's Settlement Trusts* [1987] Ch 264). There is some authority to support the view that the beneficiaries should succeed even if it could only be shown that Harold Babble had in his possession all the facts from which a reasonable person would have worked out that there was a trust and a wrong use of trust funds but he did not work this out (*Polly Peck International plc* v *Nadir (No. 2)* [1992] 4 All ER 769, *Agip (Africa) Ltd* v *Jackson* [1991] Ch 547).

9.   It is hard to give any indications of prospects of success against Harold Babble without more information although it is appreciated that it is difficult to gather information about a potential defendant's state of mind. If Mrs Babble can provide any more details it would of course be most helpful. It would also be useful if the clients or their father can be asked about how much Harold as a relative knew about the existence and terms of the trust.

10. If the trustees and Harold Babble do not seem likely to be in a position to repair the damage to the trust then it may be worth considering a tracing claim against the £10,000 transferred by Mr Babble to one and then it appears a second company of the same name. Again it is likely that the company will raise a defence that it was a bona fide business transaction. On the face of it such a defence has a greater chance of success than one raised by Harold Babble. Before advising further on this point I would need to see some more evidence as to the exact set up of the second company, the degree of influence exerted by Harold Babble and if possible more detail concerning the circumstances of the transfer. Mrs Babble may be able to provide some information on these matters.

11. If the transaction was not a bona fide business transaction for value, the beneficiaries could recover any of their original £10,000 which remains in the bank account without having to establish any degree of knowledge of a breach of trust on the part of the second company. However, this tracing remedy against an innocent volunteer is very limited and will be of no use if the bank account has some of the company's own money in and if payments have been made out of the account since the trust money was paid in.

12. If there is a very close connection between the company and Harold Babble then in my opinion if it can be established that Harold Babble was a constructive trustee then the second company will be liable as constructive trustees as well. The tracing remedy will be successful against the company as constructive trustees provided that the balance in the account since the trust money was paid in has never fallen below £10,000. If it has at any point then the beneficiaries will only be able to recover the amount which represents the lowest balance the account fell to (*Re Hallett* (1880) 13 ChD 696, *Re Tilley's Will Trusts* [1967] Ch 1179).

13. If the Fairbrothers wish to consider pursuing claims against Harold Babble and the company, it would be advisable as a first step to write to the company informing them of the situation. This will mean that at least the company will be constructive trustees of any money found to belong to the trust from the date they receive the letter. If there is any information to indicate that Harold Babble and the company were more heavily involved in the breach of trust or are about to dissipate the money to avoid the beneficiaries' claims, injunctive relief could be considered.

14. I would be happy to advise further once Adam and Chloe Fairbrother have had a chance to consider whether they wish to pursue a claim against their uncle and the company and any further information as requested above is available.

A BARRISTER

Gray's Inn

### 6.6.1.8   Appointment and removal of trustees
The first place to look to see who should appoint or remove new trustees is in the trust instrument. If no one is given such powers then the power rests with the continuing trustees by virtue of the Trustee Act 1925, s. 36. The court has power to appoint or remove trustees under the Trustee Act 1925, s. 41. Unless the beneficaries have been given powers in the trust deed they cannot generally force trustees to retire or appoint new ones although they can apply to court under s. 41. The limited exception is provided by ss. 19 and 20 of the 1996 Act. These powers to direct trustees to retire or to appoint new ones seem very far reaching but they only apply where all the beneficaries are of full age and capacity and between them beneficially entitled.

## 6.6.2 DUTIES OF TRUSTEES

The following checklist inevitably involves simplification and generalisation. It is not to be used to find answers to problems, but rather to suggest starting points on which to base fact management and legal research plans.

The trustees are each subject to a general duty to act as a prudent man of business: *Speight* v *Gaunt* (1884) 9 App Cas 1.

Duties can be enforced by the court, and a breach of duty is liable to a claim by a beneficiary.

### 6.6.2.1 Collection of assets on appointment

On accepting appointment, a trustee has a duty to ensure that all assets that should form part of the trust property pass into the hands of the trustees. Legal ownership of land, shares, etc. should be properly made over. Any appropriate legal claim to recover property should be taken, unless such claim is likely to prove fruitless. Any appropriate lists of trust property should be drawn up, and any doubts as to what should be in the trust clarified, with application to the court if necessary.

There is a continuing duty to ensure that any property which should pass into the trust does so.

Advice may be required for:

(a) a settlor — to consider what assets should be put into the trust;

(b) a trustee — to consider what assets should be in the trust, and what the chances are of recovering them;

(c) a beneficiary — to consider what property the trustees should have recovered for the trust, and whether they have done what they reasonably could to obtain it.

### 6.6.2.2 Investment

It is vital for a barrister to have general practical knowledge of what types of investment are available and what sort of return each produces, as this can be relevant in many types of case. It is the duty of a trustee to invest trust assets properly.

*Meaning of investment*

To invest involves using the capital assets of the trust to produce income or profit. This can result in problems with the capital assets that do not produce income, such as antiques, which may not automatically qualify as an 'investment' in the legal sense without special provision.

The duty to invest also involves balancing the maintenance of capital with the production of income, to be fair to all the beneficiaries. For example, a tenant for life will be entitled to income and a remainderman to capital, and both must be protected.

In making investments, the general duty is to act as a prudent man or woman of business would act if investing for persons for whom they feel morally obliged to provide: see *Cowan* v *Scargill* [1985] Ch 270. There is no duty to make the best possible investment. Subject to the terms of the trust, the duty to invest properly is continuous during the life of the trust.

*Powers in the trust instrument*

It is common for a trust instrument to specify powers of investment. It has become relatively common to give trustees wide powers, for example, to invest 'as if they were absolute owners' or 'as they see fit'. Such powers give the trustees a wide discretion, but may make it more difficult for beneficiaries to take action when the power of trustees is so wide. However, having such wide powers does not absolve trustees from exercising their powers prudently.

Where an express power of investment is provided by the trust instrument that will govern the situation, statutory powers are only implied where there is no express provision.

*Statutory powers*
To the extent that there are no express powers in the trust instrument, investment powers are implied by the Trustee Investments Act 1961, which will apply where no contrary intention is expressed. You should be generally familiar with the provisions of this Act.

The 1961 Act broadly provides that trust assets should be invested in relatively 'safe', narrow-range investments, or that they may be divided into two parts, narrow range and wider range. These two parts must be kept separate from that time on. If there are special powers in the trust instrument for part of the trust property (but not all of it), then the fund must be divided into three parts, narrow range, wider range and special range.

The first schedule to the Act lists:

(a) investments that may be made without advice (part I of the Act);

(b) investments that require advice (part II);

(c) wider-range investments, e.g. shares, unit trusts (part III).

As making investments requires some expertise, the Act also provides for trustees to seek appropriate advice. For parts II and III the trustees must obtain and consider written advice from a suitable, qualified person.

There are some special statutory rules for particular types of investment, e.g. for mortgages: TA 1925, s. 8.

The Trustee Investments (Division of Trust Fund) Order 1996 (SI 1996/845) extends the proportion of investments which can be invested in the wider-range investments from a half to three quarters. A draft Deregulation (Trustee Investments) Order 1997 proposes more sweeping changes by abolishing the restriction on wider-range investments altogether, removing the restrictions on the types of shares which can be invested in and abolishing the requirement to seek advice in respect of certain types of investment. At the time of writing there appears to be no immediate prospect of this Order being brought into force.

Under the Trusts of Land and Appointment of Trustees Act 1996 trustees of land are given an express power to purchase land for, among other purposes, investment.

**6.6.2.3 Retaining investments**
The duty regarding proper investment is continuous, so trustees should review investments at reasonable intervals. Unauthorised investments must be sold, and investments which have become unsatisfactory due to poor capital or income performance should be sold, applying the prudent man or woman of business test.

*Problems with investment powers*
With ever-widening possibilities for investment, it is possible that the powers provided by a trust instrument or by statute may prove inadequate. The first step should be to consider carefully the ambit of the powers of investment that the trustees have. If they do not permit the acquisition of a particular investment, then the trustees may seek the approval of the court for a particular transaction under TA 1925, s. 57. The court has shown itself open to extending trustees' powers where appropriate: see *Mason v Farbrother* [1983] 2 All ER 1078. In some cases a variation of trusts application may be an appropriate alternative.

Again, your client may be from one of three categories:

    (a)    Settlors: consider what powers of investment should be given to the trustees.

    (b)    Trustees: analyse clearly:

        (i)    what the powers of investment are in a particular case;

        (ii)    whether a particular investment may be made;

        (iii)    whether an application to court may be required.

    (c)    Beneficiaries: analyse whether the trustees have fulfilled their duty to invest properly, and whether they have acted within their powers. If they have not, identify clearly the breaches and resulting loss.

### 6.6.2.4 Duty to convert

Subject to the express terms of a trust, the trustees have a general duty to convert. This means that trust funds should not be left in an unproductive property — this should be sold and the proceeds properly invested. There is a general duty to convert in the case of personalty.

### 6.6.2.5 Distribution

A trustee has a duty to distribute capital and income to the right beneficiary at the right time. The question of who should be paid and when is determined by the careful interpretation of the terms of the trust.

Often the trustees are given a discretion as to the payment of capital and/or income. Such a discretion must be fairly exercised. Where there is difficulty in deciding which beneficiary to distribute to, the trustees may, as appropriate, seek the assistance of the court in the interpretation of powers, or may advertise for beneficiaries to come forward: TA 1925, s. 27.

Advice may be required as follows:

    (a)    Settlors: ensure terms as to entitlement are clearly expressed.

    (b)    Trustees: advise on the entitlement of beneficiaries, and on an application to court if appropriate — for example, if there is any doubt as to the rights of beneficiaries.

    (c)    Beneficiaries: advise on entitlement according to the terms of the trust, and on an action for breach of trust if it is alleged assets have been wrongly distributed or not distributed.

### 6.6.2.6 Equal treatment of beneficiaries

The trustee has a duty to act fairly and equally as between different beneficiaries, and as between different classes of beneficiaries. This does not mean that where there is a discretion the trustees should give all beneficiaries an equal amount, simply that they should act fairly and should at least consider whether their discretion should be exercised.

### 6.6.2.7 Duty not to profit

There is an absolute duty for a trustee not to profit from a trust. This duty has three aspects:

    (a)    A trustee is not entitled to remuneration unless this is specifically provided for by the trust document or by statute (as in the case of a judicial trustee). A professional trustee, such as a bank or a solicitor, will normally require that provision be made for remuneration.

    (b)    A trustee cannot normally buy or otherwise acquire trust property: *Keech* v *Sandford* (1726) Sel Cas t King 61. There are exceptions: for example, where the trustee is also a beneficiary; where the beneficiaries are all of age and consent; or when the approval of the court is given.

(c) A trustee cannot benefit indirectly from his position as trustee. If he does, he will be liable to account for any profit made: *Boardman* v *Phipps* [1967] 2 AC 46.

The rule does not prevent a person being named as a beneficiary and a trustee and benefiting from his position as a beneficiary.

In advising, the following points must be considered:

(a) Settlors: ensure that proper provision is made to remunerate trustees.

(b) Trustees: advise clearly on the extent of the duty not to profit.

(c) Beneficiaries: check whether there is any breach of trust, and if so, what may be sought as a result — for example, an account of profits or that property be traced.

### 6.6.2.8 Provision of accounts and information
Trustees have a duty to keep suitable accounts and produce them to a beneficiary when required. It is common practice for beneficiaries to be provided with copies of accounts, but there is no duty to provide copies, and the beneficiary may be required to pay for a copy. Accounts do not have to be audited, but a beneficiary or trustee can ask for accounts to be audited: TA 1925, ss. 22 and 13.

There is a duty to keep trust documents available for inspection by beneficiaries. These should include written records of the decisions of trustees affecting the trust. However, trustees do not have to keep records of the reasons for an exercise of discretion, and beneficiaries are not entitled to such details: *Re Londonderry's Settlement* [1965] Ch 918.

### 6.6.2.9 Duty to act unanimously
This duty is linked to the joint and several liability of trustees. An action can only be taken if all trustees agree, and all trustees are prima facie liable for any action taken unless there is permissible delegation. Charity trustees are different — they can act by a majority.

### 6.6.3 POWERS OF TRUSTEES

The powers of trustees are subject to their duties, and are primarily subject to and laid down by the trust instrument. Statute provides for general powers, but these can usually be modified or excluded by a trust instrument.

### 6.6.3.1 Powers given by the trust instrument
Note that there are different types of powers:

(a) Trustees may have decisive powers to take decisions. These may take any form directed by the trust instrument, including, for example, a power to decide who qualifies as a beneficiary: see *Re Tuck's Settlement Trusts* [1978] Ch 49.

(b) Trustees may have a discretionary power. This may relate, for example, to how much capital or income a beneficiary should get. An exercise of discretion by a trustee is difficult to challenge. Although trustees must exercise a discretion justly and fairly, they do not normally have to explain or justify their decisions.

### 6.6.3.2 Sale
For assets other than land, a power to sell will normally be implied even if it is not expressly granted by the trust instrument: TA 1925, s. 12.

The trustees should obtain the best price reasonably available on sale, acting as prudent men or women of business. Trustees have power to give a valid receipt on sale:

TA 1925, s. 14. In the case of land a receipt is not valid unless given by two trustees or a trust corporation.

### 6.6.3.3 Delegation

Trustees will often require advice and assistance, especially if they are not professional trustees, for example, with regard to valuation and legal matters. To this end, trustees have a general power to appoint agents, provided that they act as prudent men or women of business, which involves:

(a) using proper care in selecting an agent;

(b) selecting an agent with appropriate expertise;

(c) properly supervising the agent.

The power to appoint agents is specified by TA 1925, s. 23, which provides:

*(1) Trustees or personal representatives may, instead of acting personally, employ and pay an agent, whether a solicitor, banker, stockbroker, or other person, to transact any business or do any act required to be transacted or done in the execution of the trust, or the administration of the testator's or intestate's estate, including the receipt and payment of money, and shall be entitled to be allowed and paid all charges and expenses so incurred, and shall not be responsible for the default of any such agent if employed in good faith.*

*(2) Trustees or personal representatives may appoint any person to act as their agent or attorney for the purpose of selling, converting, collecting, getting in, and executing and perfecting insurances of, or managing or cultivating, or otherwise administering any property, real or personal, moveable or immoveable, subject to the trust or forming part of the testator's or intestate's estate, in any place outside the United Kingdom or executing or exercising any discretion or trust or power vested in them in relation to any such property, with such ancillary powers, and with and subject to such provisions and restrictions as they may think fit, including a power to appoint substitutes, and shall not, by reason only of their having made such appointment, be responsible for any loss arising thereby.*

*(3) Without prejudice to such general power of appointing agents as aforesaid—*

*(a) A trustee may appoint a solicitor to be his agent to receive and give a discharge for any money or valuable consideration or property receivable by the trustee under the trust, by permitting the solicitor to have the custody of, and to produce, a deed having in the body thereof or endorsed thereon a receipt for such money or valuable consideration or property, the deed being executed, or the endorsed receipt being signed, by the person entitled to give a receipt for that consideration;*

*(b) A trustee shall not be chargeable with breach of trust by reason only of his having made or concurred in making any such appointment, and the production of any such deed by the solicitor shall have the same statutory validity and effect as if the person appointing the solicitor had not been a trustee;*

*(c) A trustee may appoint a banker or solicitor to be his agent to receive and give a discharge for any money payable to the trustee under or by virtue of a policy of insurance, by permitting the banker or solicitor to have the custody of and to produce the policy of insurance with a receipt signed by the trustee, and a trustee shall not be chargeable with a breach of trust by reason only of his having made or concurred in making any such appointment:*

*Provided that nothing in this subsection shall exempt a trustee from any liability which he would have incurred if this Act and any enactment replaced by this Act had not been passed, in case he permits any such money, valuable consideration, or property to remain in the hands or under the control of the banker or solicitor for a period longer than is reasonably necessary to enable the banker or solicitor, as the case may be, to pay or transfer the same to the trustee.*

*This subsection applies whether the money or valuable consideration or property was or is received before or after the commencement of this Act.*

When an agent is appointed, there are limits on the liability of a trustee, though it may be difficult to establish where the line should be drawn: see *Re Vickery* [1931] 1 Ch 572. Limits on the liability of a trustee appear in TA 1925, ss. 23 and 30. Section 30 states:

> *(1) A trustee shall be chargeable only for money and securities actually received by him notwithstanding his signing any receipt for the sake of conformity, and shall be answerable and accountable only for his own acts, receipts, neglects, or defaults, and not for those of any other trustee, nor for any banker, broker, or other person with whom any trust money or securities may be deposited, nor for the insufficiency or deficiency of any securities, nor for any other loss, unless the same happens through his own wilful default.*
>
> *(2) A trustee may reimburse himself or pay or discharge out of the trust premises all expenses incurred in or about the execution of the trusts or powers.*

In advising a trustee, give clear advice about the appointment of agents, and the extent of liability for their actions. In advising a beneficiary, consider carefully the possible liability of trustees and agents.

(Note that where delegation has occurred, it may be possible: to sue the trustee; to sue the agent; to argue that the agent should be held to be a constructive trustee of property; or to trace trust property.)

### 6.6.3.4 Maintenance

Maintenance powers concern the income of a trust. Until a capital interest vests, it should be clear what happens to income. The basic possibilities are:

(a) that a beneficiary is entitled to income (e.g. a tenant for life);

(b) that trustees have a discretion to give income to beneficiaries;

(c) that income is accumulated in the trust.

The maintenance powers for a particular trust may be specified in the trust instrument or may be implied by statute. The powers under TA 1925, s. 31 apply unless they are excluded:

> *(1) Where any property is held by trustees in trust for any person for any interest whatsoever, whether vested or contingent, then, subject to any prior interests or charges affecting that property —*
> *(i) during the infancy of any such person, if his interest so long continues, the trustees may, at their sole discretion, pay to his parent or guardian, if any, or otherwise apply for or towards his maintenance, education, or benefit, the whole or such part, if any, of the income of that property as may, in all the circumstances, be reasonable, whether or not there is—*
> *(a) any other fund applicable to the same purpose; or*
> *(b) any person bound by law to provide for his maintenance or education; and*
> *(ii) if such person on attaining the age of [eighteen years] has not a vested interest in such income, the trustees shall thenceforth pay the income of that property and of any accretion thereto under subsection (2) of this section to him, until he either attains a vested interest therein or dies, or until failure of his interest:*
> *Provided that, in deciding whether the whole or any part of the income of the property is during a minority to be paid or applied for the purposes aforesaid, the trustees shall have regard to the age of the infant and his requirements and generally to the circumstances of the case, and in particular to what other income, if any, is applicable for the same purposes; and where trustees have notice that the income of more than one fund is applicable for those purposes, then, so far as practicable, unless the entire income of the funds is paid or applied as aforesaid or the court otherwise directs, a proportionate part only of the income of each fund shall be so paid or applied.*
> *(2) During the infancy of any such person, if his interest so long continues, the trustees shall accumulate all the residue of that income in the way of compound*

*interest by investing the same and the resulting income thereof from time to time in authorised investments, and shall hold those accumulations as follows:—*

*(i)    If any such person—*

*(a)    attains the age of [eighteen years], or marries under that age, and his interest in such income during his infancy or until his marriage is a vested interest; or*

*(b)    on attaining the age of [eighteen years] or on marriage under that age becomes entitled to the property from which such income arose in fee simple, absolute or determinable, or absolutely, or for an entailed interest:*

*the trustees shall hold the accumulations in trust for such person absolutely, but without prejudice to any provision with respect thereto contained in any settlement by him made under any statutory powers during his infancy, and so that the receipt of such person after marriage, and though still an infant, shall be a good discharge; and*

*(ii)    In any other case the trustees shall, notwithstanding that such person had a vested interest in such income, hold the accumulations as an accretion to the capital of the property from which such accumulations arose, and as one fund with such capital for all purposes, and so that, if such property is settled land, such accumulations shall be held upon the same trusts as if the same were capital money arising therefrom:*

*but the trustees may, at any time during the infancy of such person if his interest so long continues, apply those accumulations, or any part thereof, as if they were income arising in the then current year.*

*(3)    This section applies in the case of a contingent interest only if the limitation or trust carries the intermediate income of the property, but it applies to a future or contingent legacy by the parent of, or a person standing in loco parentis to, the legatee, if and for such period as, under the general law, the legacy carries interest for the maintenance of the legatee, and in any such case as last aforesaid the rate of interest shall (if the income available is sufficient, and subject to any rules of court to the contrary) be five pounds per centum per annum.*

Advice may be required on these matters:

(a)    Settlors: consider what powers of maintenance should be provided.

(b)    Trustees: establish what the powers of maintenance are for the particular trust, including what entitlements there are and where discretion lies.

(c)    Beneficiaries: establish what the powers of maintenance are for the particular trust, and whether the particular beneficiary has a specific or a discretionary entitlement. If entitlement is discretionary, the trustees only have to consider providing maintenance.

### 6.6.3.5    Advancement

Powers of advancement relate to the capital of a trust. The terms of a trust should clearly specify when capital will vest for a beneficiary. The basic possibilities are:

(a)    that a beneficiary becomes entitled to capital on reaching a specified age, or fulfilling a specified condition;

(b)    that trustees have a discretion when to give capital to a beneficiary.

Powers to advance capital to a beneficiary before full entitlement arises under the trust may be provided by the trust instrument or may be implied by TA 1925, s. 32, which applies unless it is excluded:

*(1)    Trustees may at any time or times pay or apply any capital money subject to a trust, for the advancement or benefit, in such manner as they may, in their absolute discretion, think fit, of any, person entitled to the capital of the trust property or of any share thereof, whether absolutely or contingently on his attaining any specified age or on the occurrence of any other event, or subject to a gift over on his death under any specified age or on the occurrence of any other event, and whether in possession*

*or in remainder or reversion, and such payment or application may be made notwithstanding that the interest of such person is liable to be defeated by the exercise of a power of appointment or revocation, or to be diminished by the increase of the class to which he belongs:*

*Provided that—*

*(a) the money so paid or applied for the advancement or benefit of any person shall not exceed altogether in amount one-half of the presumptive or vested share or interest of that person in the trust property; and*

*(b) if that person is or becomes absolutely and indefeasibly entitled to a share in the trust property the money so paid or applied shall be brought into account as part of such share; and*

*(c) no such payment or application shall be made so as to prejudice any person entitled to any prior life or other interest, whether vested or contingent, in the money paid or applied unless such person is in existence and of full age and consents in writing to such payment or application.*

*(2) This section applies only where the trust property consists of money or securities or property held upon trust for sale calling in and conversion, and such money or securities, or the proceeds of such sale calling in and conversion are not by statute or in equity considered as land, or applicable as capital money for the purposes of the Settled Land Act, 1925.*

*(3) This section does not apply to trusts constituted or created before the commencement of this Act.*

Advising on advancement may involve the following:

(a) Settlors: consider what terms for entitlement and advancement should be included.

(b) Trustees: establish what the terms of entitlement and advancement are for a particular trust, including where any discretion lies.

(c) Beneficiaries: establish what the entitlement of the particular beneficiary is, and what powers of advancement there are. If there is a discretion to advance, the trustees only have to consider making an advancement.

### 6.6.3.6 Administrative powers

Trustees need appropriate powers to administer the trust. Primarily such powers can be provided by the trust instrument, but some administrative powers are provided by statute:

(a) Insurance. Trustees have no absolute duty to insure property but should act as prudent men or women of business. A power to insure is contained in TA 1925, s. 19.

(b) Compounding liabilities. Trustees have a power to settle debts on behalf of the trust: TA 1925, s. 15.

### 6.6.3.7 Costs and expenses

Trustees have a power to seek reimbursement for the costs and expenses of administrating a trust, that is, to have such expenses paid from the trust funds: TA 1925, s. 30(2). The expense of legal proceedings regarding a trust will normally be met from the trust funds unless a court orders otherwise.

## 6.7 Checklist for Cases Involving Testamentary Provisions

(a) Does the document appear to be intended to take effect on the death of the settlor and has the settlor died? If so then the document must be treated as a testamentary disposition.

(b) If you are not acting for the executors has the document been admitted to probate? If it has, challenge is much harder; see further **7.2.6**.

(c)   Is there another document in existence drawn up by the settlor which appears to be intended to take effect on the death of the settlor? If so and it post-dates your document, can it be read as a codicil to yours, or if it pre-dates yours, can yours be read as a codicil to the earlier one?

(d)   Does the intended will comply with the legal formalities? In particular:

   (i)    Is it signed?

   (ii)   Is it properly witnessed?

(e)   Is there any doubt about the capacity of the testator to make a will?

(f)   Is there any doubt about the genuineness of the signatures or the will itself?

(g)   Is there any evidence of undue influence?

(h)   Is it clear who the executors and/or trustees are and are they able and willing to act?

(i)   Is it clear who the beneficiaries are intended to be and are they traceable and willing to accept the gift?

(j)   Are all the provisions clear and unambiguous on their face?

(k)   Does the meaning of any provision become less clear when other evidence is considered?

(l)   Are the provisions where the meaning is clear lawfully possible to give effect to e.g., will purporting to dispose of property overseas?

(m)   If someone wishes to challenge the will, does he have standing to do so?

(n)   Even if no one wants to challenge the will, should the executors seek the assistance of the court?

(o)   Is there anyone who may have a claim under the Inheritance (Provision for Family and Dependants) Act 1975?

(p)   If the will has been admitted to probate, are there doubts about how the estate is being dealt with? If so, have the executors completed the administration of the estate? If they have and there is a doubt about the way trusts under the will are being administered, apply the trusts checklist below. If not, consider the duties of executors.

# 6.8    Checklist for Trusts

(a)   Is there a document which purports to have the intention to create a trust obligation?

(b)   If not, can a trust obligation be implied from other circumstances or by operation of law?

(c)   Is the property intended to be covered by the trust obligation in existence and clearly defined?

(d)   Is the subject matter of the trust land or is any interest in land included in the property?

(e)   Is it clear who the trustees are intended to be and are they all able and willing to act?

(f)   If there are no trustees or the number able and willing to act fall below a minimum number of trustees specified in the trust document, who has the power to appoint trustees?

(g)   Is it clear who the beneficiaries are intended to be? Are any potential beneficiaries minors, unascertained, acting under a disability, or not traceable?

(h)   If the trust is intended to be charitable, is it registered? Are the objects clear and lawful?

(i)   If there is a trust document does the meaning of the provisions appear clear from the document?

    (i)   First construe the document using any appropriate canons of construction.

    (ii)   Next see if the provision in question has been the subject of judicial interpretation.

    (iii)   Then see if there is any special extraneous evidence which sheds light on the meaning of the words used in the particular case.

(j)   If there is no document, what rights and duties are implied by law?

(k)   Are the provisions in the document lawfully possible to give effect to?

(l)   Are the provisions in the document supplemented, altered or superseded by statutory provisions or principles derived from case law or, in the case of a charitable trust, directions given by the Charity Commissioners?

(m)   If the provisions are clear, can they be altered?

(n)   If the provisions are clear, is there any doubt about the way they are being administered?

(o)   Does the doubt involve the dispositive or administrative provisions?

(p)   Does the doubt involve the exercise of discretionary powers or mandatory duties?

(q)   If there is concern about possible wrongdoing by trustees, are immediate measures needed to protect the trust?

(r)   If there is a potential challenge, who exactly is or are your client or clients? Is there any possible conflict of interest?

(s)   Does a person seeking to challenge the provisions or operation of a trust have standing to do so?

(t)   Even if there is no dispute, should the trustees be seeking the assistance of the court?

(u)   Who should be included in any intended proceedings? What can be done if any are not traceable?

# SEVEN

# PROVISION ON DEATH

## 7.1    Introduction

Apart from checking the form and content of any purported testamentary disposition certain other issues need to be considered when called upon to advise on the death of a property owner.

### 7.1.1    INTESTACY

If the deceased did not leave a will, his estate will devolve following the statutory rules of intestacy under the Administration of Estates Act 1925. The rules apply not only if there is an intestacy regarding the whole estate, but also if there is a partial intestacy, for example if a term of the will fails. The devolution of assets depends on which relatives survive the deceased. The rules can only be modified by court order for provision: see **7.1.2**. Inheritance tax liability can arise under the normal rules where there is an intestacy.

For convenience, the provisions for intestacy are summarised in **Table 7.1**.

### 7.1.2    ORDERS FOR PROVISION

The terms of a will or the rules of intestacy will primarily dictate the distribution of assets on death. However, the result of this may be to make inadequate provision for a spouse, child or cohabitee. A person who feels that inadequate provision has been made for him may apply for provision under the Inheritance (Provision for Family and Dependants) Act 1975, as amended by the Law Reform (Succession) Act 1995, for estates of persons dying after 1 January 1996.

#### 7.1.2.1    Potential applicants
First it is necessary to decide whether the potential applicant can apply at all. Section 1 of the 1975 Act states:

> *(1)    Where after the commencement of this Act a person dies domiciled in England and Wales and is survived by any of the following persons:—*
> *(a)    the wife or husband of the deceased;*
> *(b)    a former wife or former husband of the deceased who has not remarried;*
> *(c)    a child of the deceased;*
> *(d)    any person (not being a child of the deceased) who, in the case of any marriage to which the deceased was at any time a party, was treated by the deceased as a child of the family in relation to that marriage;*
> *(e)    any person (not being a person included in the foregoing paragraphs of this subsection) who immediately before the death of the deceased was being maintained, either wholly or partly, by the deceased;*
> *that person may apply to the court for an order under section 2 of this Act on the ground that the disposition of the deceased's estate effected by his will or the law relating to intestacy, or the combination of his will and that law, is not such as to make reasonable financial provision for that applicant.*

**Table 7.1 Distribution on intestacy (Administration of Estates Act 1925, as amended). Deaths after 1 June 1987**

| Surviving relative(s) | Person(s) entitled to the estate | Person(s) entitled to grant of letters of administration |
|---|---|---|
| 1 Spouse only | Surviving spouse absolutely | Surviving spouse |
| 2 Spouse and issue | (a) Surviving spouse takes:<br>(i) personal chattels;<br>(ii) £75,000;<br>(iii) life interest in half residuary estate.<br>(b) Issue take residuary estate at age 18 subject to life interest in half of surviving spouse in equal shares *per stirpes*. | Surviving spouse and one other person |
| 3 Spouse and parent(s) | (a) Surviving spouse takes:<br>(i) personal chattels;<br>(ii) £125,000;<br>(iii) half residuary estate absolutely.<br>(b) Parent(s) take half residuary estate (in equal shares). | Surviving spouse |
| 4 Spouse and brother(s) and/or sister(s) of the whole blood and/or issue of such who predeceased the intestate | (a) Surviving spouse takes:<br>(i) personal chattels;<br>(ii) £125,000;<br>(iii) half residuary estate absolutely.<br>(b) Brother(s) and sister(s) and/or issue take half residuary estate at age 18 in equal shares *per stirpes*. | Surviving spouse (and one other person) |
| 5 Issue | Issue at age 18 in equal shares *per stirpes*. | Child or remoter issue (and one other person) |
| 6 Parent(s) | Parent(s) in equal shares. | Parent |
| 7 Brother(s) and/or sister(s) of the whole blood and/or issue of such who predeceased the intestate | Brother(s) and sister(s) and/or issue at age 18 in equal shares *per stirpes*. | Brother or sister or issue etc (and one other person) |
| 8 Brother(s) and/or sister(s) of the half blood and/or issue of such who predeceased the intestate | Half-brother(s) and half-sister(s) and/or issue at age 18 in equal shares *per stirpes*. | Half-brother or half-sister or issue etc. (and one other person) |
| 9 Grandparents | Grandparent(s) (in equal shares). | Grandparent |
| 10 Uncle(s) and/or aunt(s) of the whole blood and/or issue of such who predeceased the intestate | Uncle(s) and aunt(s) and/or issue at age 18 in equal shares *per stirpes*. | Uncle or aunt or issue etc. (and one other person) |
| 11 Uncle(s) and/or aunt(s) of the half blood and/or issue of such who predeceased the intestate | Such uncle(s) and aunt(s) and/or issue at age 18 in equal shares *per stirpes*. | Such uncle, aunt or issue etc. (and one other person) |
| 12 No relative as mentioned above | The Crown as *bona vacantia*. | The Crown |

An important extension is made by the Law Reform (Succession) Act 1995. Section 1 of the 1975 Act states:

*(1A) This subsection applies to a person if the deceased died on or after 1st January 1996 and, during the whole of the period of two years ending immediately before the date when the deceased died, the person was living—*
*(a) in the same household as the deceased, and*
*(b) as the husband or wife of the deceased.*

If the person can apply the application is for 'reasonable financial provision':

*(2) In this Act 'reasonable financial provision'—*
*(a) in the case of an application made by virtue of subsection (1)(a) above by the husband or wife of the deceased (except where the marriage with the deceased was the subject of a decree of judicial separation and at the date of death the decree was in force and the separation was continuing), means such financial provision as it would be reasonable in all the circumstances of the case for a husband or wife to receive, whether or not that provision is required for his or her maintenance;*
*(b) in the case of any other application made by virtue of subsection (1) above, means such financial provision as it would be reasonable in all the circumstances of the case for the applicant to receive for his maintenance.*
*(3) For the purposes of subsection (1)(e) above, a person shall be treated as being maintained by the deceased, either wholly or partly, as the case may be, if the deceased, otherwise than for full valuable consideration, was making a substantial contribution in money or money's worth towards the reasonable needs of that person.*

### 7.1.2.2 Orders available
The orders that may be made are specified in s. 2 of the 1975 Act:

*(1) Subject to the provisions of this Act, where an application is made for an order under this section, the court may, if it is satisfied that the disposition of the deceased's estate effected by his will or the law relating to intestacy, or the combination of his will and that law, is not such as to make reasonable financial provision for the applicant, make any one or more of the following orders:—*
*(a) an order for the making to the applicant out of the net estate of the deceased of such periodical payments and for such term as may be specified in the order;*
*(b) an order for the payment to the applicant out of that estate of a lump sum of such amount as may be so specified;*
*(c) an order for the transfer to the applicant of such property comprised in that estate as may be so specified;*
*(d) an order for the settlement for the benefit of the applicant of such property comprised in that estate as may be so specified;*
*(e) an order for the acquisition out of property comprised in that estate of such property as may be so specified and for the transfer of the property so acquired to the applicant or for the settlement thereof for his benefit;*
*(f) an order varying any ante-nuptial or post-nuptial settlement (including such a settlement made by will) made on the parties to a marrriage to which the deceased was one of the parties, the variation being for the benefit of the surviving party to that marriage, or any child of that marriage or any person who was treated by the deceased as a child of the family in relation to that marriage.*
*(2) An order under subsection (1)(a) above providing for the making out of the net estate of the deceased of periodical payments may provide for—*
*(a) payments of such amount as may be specified in the order,*
*(b) payments equal to the whole of the income of the net estate or such portion thereof as may be so specified,*
*(c) payments equal to the whole of the income of such part of the net estate as the court may direct to be set aside or appropriated for the making out of the income thereof of payments under this section,*
*or may provide for the amount of the payments or any of them to be determinined in any other way the court thinks fit.*
*(3) Where an order under subsection (1)(a) above provides for the making of payments of an amount specified in the order, the order may direct that such part of*

*the net estate as may be so specified shall be set aside or appropriated for the making out of the income thereof of those payments; but no larger part of the net estate shall be so set aside or appropriated than is sufficient, at the date of the order, to produce by the income thereof the amount required for the making of those payments.*

*(4)   An order under this section may contain such consequential and supplemental provisions as the court thinks necessary or expedient for the purpose of giving effect to the order or for the purpose of securing that the order operates fairly as between one beneficiary of the estate of the deceased and another and may, in particular, but without prejudice to the generality of this subsection—*

*(a)   order any person who holds any property which forms part of the net estate of the deceased to make such payment or transfer such property as may be specified in the order;*

*(b)   vary the disposition of the deceased's estate effected by the will or the law relating to intestacy, or by both the will and the law relating to intestacy, in such manner as the court thinks fair and reasonable having regard to the provision of the order and all the circumstances of the case;*

*(c)   confer on the trustees of any property which is the subject of an order under this section such powers as appear to the court to be necessary or expedient.*

### 7.1.2.3   Matters to be considered

If an application can be considered, certain factors have to be had regard to in all cases. Section 3 of the 1975 Act states:

*(1)   Where an application is made for an order under section 2 of this Act, the court shall, in determining whether the disposition of the deceased's estate effected by his will or the law relating to intestacy, or the combination of his will and that law, is such as to make reasonable financial provision for the applicant and, if the court considers that reasonable financial provision has not been made, in determining whether and in what manner it shall exercise its powers under that section, have regard to the following matters, that is to say—*

*(a)   the financial resources and financial needs which the applicant has or is likely to have in the foreseeable future;*

*(b)   the financial resources and financial needs which any other applicant for an order under section 2 of this Act has or is likely to have in the foreseeable future;*

*(c)   the financial resources and financial needs which any beneficiary of the estate of the deceased has or is likely to have in the foreseeable future;*

*(d)   any obligations and responsibilities which the deceased had towards any applicant for an order under the said section 2 or towards any beneficiary of the estate of the deceased;*

*(e)   the size and nature of the net estate of the deceased;*

*(f)   any physical or mental disability of any applicant for an order under the said section 2 or any beneficiary of the estate of the deceased;*

*(g)   any other matter, including the conduct of the applicant or any other person, which in the circumstances of the case the court may consider relevant.*

Other factors are to be applied to cases in specific categories:

*(2)   Without prejudice to the generality of paragraph (g) of subsection (1) above, where an application for an order under section 2 of this Act is made by virtue of section 1(1)(a) or 1(1)(b) of this Act, the court shall, in addition to the matters specifically mentioned in paragraphs (a) to (f) of that subsection, have regard to—*

*(a)   the age of the applicant and the duration of the marriage,*

*(b)   the contribution made by the applicant to the welfare of the family of the deceased, including any contribution made by looking after the home or caring for the family;*

*and, in the case of an application by the wife or husband of the deceased, the court shall also, unless at the date of death a decree of judicial separation was in force and the separation was continuing, have regard to the provision which the applicant might reasonably have expected to receive if on the day on which the deceased died the marriage, instead of being terminated by death, had been terminated by a decree of divorce.*

*(3) Without prejudice to the generality of paragraph (g) of subsection (1) above, where an application for an order under section 2 of this Act is made by virtue of section 1(1)(c) or 1(1)(d) of this Act, the court shall, in addition to the matters specifically mentioned in paragraphs (a) to (f) of that subsection, have regard to the manner in which the applicant was being or in which he might expect to be educated or trained, and where the application is made by virtue of section 1(1)(d) the court shall also have regard—*

*(a)  to whether the deceased had assumed any responsibility for the applicant's maintenance and, if so, to the extent to which and the basis upon which the deceased assumed that responsibility and to the length of time for which the deceased discharged that responsibility;*

*(b)  to whether in assuming and discharging that responsibility the deceased did so knowing that the applicant was not his own child;*

*(c)  to the liability of any other person to maintain the applicant.*

*(4)  Without prejudice to the generality of paragraph (g) of subsection (1) above, where an application for an order under section 2 of this Act is made by virtue of section 1(1)(e) of this Act, the court shall, in addition to the matters specifically mentioned in paragraphs (a) to (f) of that subsection, have regard to the extent to which and the basis upon which the deceased assumed responsibility for the maintenance of the applicant and to the length of time for which the deceased discharged that responsibility.*

*(5)  In considering the matters to which the court is required to have regard under this section, the court shall take into account the facts as known to the court at the date of the hearing.*

*(6)  In considering the financial resources of any person for the purposes of this section the court shall take into account his earning capacity and in considering the financial needs of any person for the purposes of this section the court shall take into account his financial obligations and responsibilities.*

Under the 1995 Act an additional set of factors must be taken into account:

*(2A)  Without prejudice to the generality of paragraph (g) of subsection (1) above, where an application for an order under section 2 of this Act is made by virtue of section 1(1)(ba) of this Act, the court shall, in addition to the matters specifically mentioned in paragraphs (a) to (f) of that subsection, have regard to—*

*(a)  the age of the applicant and the length of the period during which the applicant lived as the husband or wife of the deceased and in the same household as the deceased;*

*(b)  the contribution made by the applicant to the welfare of the family of the deceased, including any contribution made by looking after the home or caring for the family.*

**7.1.2.4  Case law**

There is substantial case law on the application of the Act. There are a number of cases on the procedural requirements, especially applications to extend the time limit for applying. Generally, the courts are not keen to grant extensions for long delays where other beneficiaries or applicants would be prejudiced. But in *Stock v Brown* [1994] 1 FLR 840 a six-year delay was excused. See also *Re W (a minor)* [1995] 2 FCR 689 in relation to child applicants seeking time extensions. On the substantive provision, it is clear, for example, that a widow can seek provision even if she has been separated from her husband for some years: *Re Rowlands* [1984] FLR 813; or even if she has specifically been left out of the will: *Dawkins v Judd* [1986] 2 FLR 360. As regards claims which effectively oppose the claims of other relatives — a wife will not be forced to sell a house to provide for children: *Rajabally v Rajabally* [1987] 2 FLR 390; and the wife will tend to get some provision if assets have been left to more distant relatives: *Kusminow v Barclays Bank Trust Co.* [1989] Fam Law 66. Claims for children will generally be sympathetically received even if the child was not being supported at the time of death: *Re Leach* [1986] Ch 226. However, a claim may be rejected if the child has been very disruptive and difficult: *Williams v Johns* [1988] 2 FLR 475. Failure to support a child during infancy was not held to be a factor in deciding whether reasonable provision had been made for a child: *Re Jennings* [1994] Ch 286, CA.

The test for what is reasonable is objective, but what might have been ordered on divorce is relevant: *Moody* v *Stevenson* [1992] Ch 486. However, especially in the case of small estates the starting point of what might have been obtained on a divorce may not be helpful: *Re Krubert* [1997] Ch 97, CA. It should, however, be decided that reasonable provision has not been made before the right amount is considered: *Jessop* v *Jessop* [1992] 1 FLR 591. On the position of adult children, see *Snapes* v *Aram* (1998) *The Times*, 8 May 1998.

### 7.1.2.5 Jurisdiction and procedure

Applications can be made to the county court and to either the Family or Chancery Divisions of the High Court. Under the new Civil Procedure Rules 1998 all proceedings irrespective of which court they are commenced in are governed by the re-enacted and amended RSC O. 99.

The new CPR, Part 8 procedures for commencing proceedings apply to proceedings under the 1975 Act and replace the expedited form of originating summons which was previously prescribed.

If acting for a potential claimant it should be noted that claims should be made within six months of the date of probate. The court has a discretion to disapply the time limit. The time limit under the old Rules was generally fairly rigorously applied.

Defendants who are other persons claiming entitlement under the will or intestacy should lodge a witness statement or affidavit setting out their financial circumstances for the court to take them into account in balancing the needs and resources of all relevant parties.

# 7.2 Probate

### 7.2.1 INTRODUCTORY MATTERS

The notes that follow are included in the Manual as useful background for an intending Chancery practitioner. Probate matters are routinely the province of solicitors rather than counsel, but a barrister can be asked to advise on probate issues in contentious cases (where the drafting of court proceedings may also be required) and in other situations giving rise to difficulties — a common example would be where the validity of a will is less than clear.

What follows is no more than an outline of the basic structure of probate jurisdiction. For the kind of case that typically comes before counsel, it would be necessary to go into greater detail by consulting one of the specialist sources, the main ones being Williams, Mortimer and Sunnucks, *Executors, Administrators and Probate*; Tristram and Coote, *Probate Practice*, and *Butterworth's Wills, Probate and Administration Service*. *Halsbury's Laws* Vol. 17 contains a useful section on Probate, and *Atkin's Court Forms* Vol. 32 should be consulted for drafting requirements.

### 7.2.1.1 What do we mean by probate?

A number of different legal questions or problems can arise in relation to the estate of a deceased. However, it is inappropriate to describe every such question as giving rise to a probate issue. The probate jurisdiction of the court only comes into play where the following questions are relevant:

(a) Does a particular document satisfy the requirements of a valid last will so that it can be proved as such (i.e. admitted to probate)?

(b) Who is entitled to act as personal representative and obtain a grant of probate or administration (as the case may be) in respect of the deceased person's estate?

A host of other important questions concerning the devolution or administration of an estate often arise at the same time as these, but strictly speaking these are the only questions properly described as 'probate' issues.

### 7.2.1.2 Contentious and non-contentious business

Within the probate jurisdiction of the court, there is a key distinction to be drawn between contentious or 'solemn form' business and non-contentious or 'common form' business. As these terms themselves suggest, the former covers cases where there is a dispute as to validity of a will or who should act, whereas the latter covers non-disputatious cases.

*Definition of non-contentious business*
There is a statutory definition of non-contentious or common form probate business in the Supreme Court Act 1981, s. 128, which is as follows:

> *the business of obtaining probate and administration where there is no contention as to the right thereto, including—*
> *(a)  the passing of probates and administrations through the High Court in contentious cases where the contest has been terminated,*
> *(b)  all business of a non-contentious nature in matters of testacy and intestacy not being proceedings in any action, and*
> *(c)  the business of lodging caveats against the grant of probate or administration.*

The last of the categories, involving caveats, is explained in more detail below.

*Definition of contentious business*
Contentious or solemn form business is not statutorily defined, but can generally be equated with probate actions, of which there are three main types:

(a)  Those involving a contest as to the validity of a will.

(b)  So-called 'interest actions', which turn on the question of whether a particular person is entitled to a grant of representation, i.e. probate or letters of administration.

(c)  Actions which raise the question of whether a grant of representation previously made should now be revoked.

### 7.2.1.3 Which court has jurisdiction?

All non-contentious business is dealt with by the Family Division of the High Court, which controls and administers the various probate registries and sub-registries dotted around England and Wales — for a full list of these, see *Butterworth's Probate and Administration Service*, para. D800–802.

In the High Court, contentious business is dealt with by the Chancery Division. However, the county court has jurisdiction to hear contentious cases where the net value of the estate does not exceed £30,000: County Courts Act 1984, s. 32.

### 7.2.2 PROCEDURE FOR OBTAINING A GRANT IN NON-CONTENTIOUS CASES

### 7.2.2.1 Preliminary points

A grant of probate or administration can be applied for by the executor or proposed administrator in person — it is not necessary for an *individual* personal representative to be legally represented in the application, which should be made at the most convenient probate registry (there are no venue rules governing where the application is to be made). However, where a grant is being sought by a trust corporation (e.g. a bank), the application must be made through a solicitor.

Before applying, it is necessary for the applicant to deliver an account, showing the value of the estate, to the Inland Revenue (Capital Taxes Office) for inheritance tax purposes, unless the gross value of the estate does not exceed £200,000. (Note that the figure is updated quite frequently and should be checked where relevant in a particular case.)

If inheritance tax is payable, no grant of probate or administration can be obtained until the assessment has been paid. It is sometimes necessary for the applicant to obtain a bridging loan to pay the inheritance tax.

### 7.2.2.2 The application
On applying for a grant, the applicant must produce at the probate registry:

(a)  the will, if there is one (preferably the original or an authenticated copy);

(b)  the appropriate fee for the grant — this is based on the value of the estate;

(c)  an affidavit.

The last mentioned item is very important. The form of the affidavit required will differ according to the circumstances of the case, but in all cases it is important to deal with the following matters:

(a)  The fact and date of the deceased's death.

(b)  The domicile of the deceased at the date of death — this is in case any question of recognition of the grant by a foreign court arises at a later stage.

(c)  The will or intestacy — where the applicant is seeking to prove a will, he or she must verify that the document he produces is the original last will and testament of the deceased, or an authenticated copy thereof. If there is no will, the affidavit should verify that the deceased died intestate.

(d)  The applicant must verify his entitlement to a grant of representation — see below.

(e)  The applicant must state whether, to the best of his knowledge, information and belief, the deceased was tenant for life under a Settled Land Act settlement at the date of death where the land remains settled thereafter (if this is the case the land will not pass to the deceased's ordinary personal representative, but instead the Settled Land Act trustees as special personal representatives will obtain a grant of representation limited to settled land and then be under a duty to vest the legal title in the person next entitled under the settlement to exercise the powers of tenant for life).

(f)  The applicant must swear that he will perform the duties of a personal representative in accordance with Administration of Estates Act 1925, viz.

    (i)  collect and get in the deceased's property, and then administer the estate;

    (ii)  when required by the court, draw up an inventory of the estate and give an account of the administration; and

    (iii)  when required, deliver up the grant of representation to the court.

(g)  The gross and net values of the estate.

### 7.2.2.3 Who is entitled to apply?
Where there is a will in which a person is named as executor, that person is entitled to apply for a grant of probate. If there is more than one named executor, not all those named need apply. Those who do not wish to act may either *renounce probate* or *reserve power to act*.

A renunciation should be in writing and filed at the probate registry. It may later be retracted, but only with the leave of the court.

Where a named executor reserves power to act, he or she does not apply initially for a grant, but may do so at a later stage.

If there is a will but none of the named executors is able or willing to act, or no executor is named in the will, the person entitled to a grant is the residuary beneficiary. Since such person is not named as executor in the will, it is appropriate for him to apply for a grant of administration with the will annexed to the grant, rather than for a grant of probate.

If the deceased has died intestate, the statutory next of kin are entitled to apply for a grant of administration — see Administration of Estates Act 1925, ss. 46 and 47 to ascertain next of kin in a given case.

Finally, if the applicant for a grant turns out to be someone other than the person apparently entitled to apply under the foregoing rules, the affidavit should state why the person or persons with a prior right are not applying.

### 7.2.3    EVIDENCE OF DUE EXECUTION

It is not necessary for a person seeking to prove a will to provide evidence of due execution by the deceased where the will:

(a)  contains an attestation clause, and

(b)  is not apparently irregular.

A standard form of attestation would be in the following terms:

Signed by the above-named testator XY as his last will in the presence of us both present at the same time who in his presence and in the presence of each other have hereunto subscribed our names as witnesses.

Where there is no attestation clause, or in some other respect a doubt arises as to the proper execution of the will, an *affidavit of due execution* will be required. This should be obtained, if possible, from one of the attesting witnesses; otherwise from some other person who was present when the will was signed.

If nobody is available to give such evidence, then an affidavit should be obtained from a person competent to give opinion evidence as to the genuineness of the deceased's signature.

If there is no attestation clause and it is impossible to obtain evidence of the kind outlined above, the person seeking to prove the will should rely on *the presumption of due execution*, which would apply where the appearance of the will was consistent with the proper formalities having been complied with and in the absence of contrary evidence.

### 7.2.4    ISSUE OF A GRANT OF REPRESENTATION

When a grant of probate is obtained, the probate registry will retain the original will (or authenticated copy) submitted with the application, but will issue a copy to the executor together with the grant of probate.

In the case of intestacy, the registry will issue letters of administration authorising the administrator to act as the deceased's personal representative.

Where there is a will, but the applicant is not a named executor, the registry will issue letters of administration with a copy of the will attached.

## 7.2.5    LESS STRAIGHTFORWARD CASES; CAVEATS AND CITATIONS

The foregoing is an outline of the procedure for obtaining a grant of representation in a straightforward, non-contentious case.

Before turning our attention to contentious cases, let us consider two devices which can arise in a non-contentious case and have the effect of making the position more complicated, viz. *caveats* and *citations*.

### 7.2.5.1    Caveats

A caveat is a notice in writing, which may be entered at any probate registry, the effect of which is to prevent any grant of representation being issued without the person who entered the notice (known as 'the caveator') being informed.

Once entered, a caveat is effective for six months, and is then renewable for further periods of up to six months at a time.

An index of caveats entered in all the probate registries is kept, and this has to be checked by a registrar before any grant of probate or administration is issued.

*When would a caveat be entered?*
A caveat would typically be entered in a case which showed signs of becoming contentious.

It is a device which can be used as a blocking measure by someone who intends to challenge either:

(a)   the validity of a will, or

(b)   the right of a particular person to obtain a grant.

A caveat would be especially useful where the caveator needed time to evaluate the strength of his case, or to gather evidence, before initiating proceedings. For the form of a caveat, see Non-Contentious Probate Rules 1987, sch. 1, form 3.

Once a probate action has been commenced, the caveat is, strictly speaking, no longer necessary because the effect of initiating proceedings is to prevent any grant of representation being issued.

*Challenging a caveat*
When a person wishes to apply for a grant and finds that he or she is unable to do so because of a caveat, it is possible to challenge the caveat by issuing *a warning* to the caveator. For form, see Non-Contentious Probate Rules 1987, sch. 1, form 4.

A warning should state the interest in the matter of the applicant and set out the courses of action open to the caveator, viz. either:

(a)   to enter an appearance to the warning, or

(b)   to issue a summons for directions.

The caveator has eight days in which to respond to the warning: if he does nothing within that time, the caveat ceases to be effective, and a grant of representation may then be issued to the applicant.

If the caveator enters an appearance to the warning, no grant can subsequently be issued without an order of the court. For form of appearance to warning, see Non-Contentious Probate Rules 1987, sch. 1, form 5.

It is only possible for a caveator to enter an appearance if his interest in the matter is contrary to that of the person issuing the warning, e.g. where the caveator claims to be an executor under a valid will and the person warning claims to be entitled to letters of administration on the grounds that the will is invalid.

The caveator should issue a summons for directions in a case where his interest in the estate is not contrary to that of the person warning, e.g., each of them may be statutory next of kin of an intestate. The reason for the summons for directions in such a case would be to show why the person warning should not obtain a grant.

### 7.2.5.2 Citations

A citation is an order issued by the Principal Registry of the Family Division calling on the party cited to show cause why a particular step — usually application for a grant — should not be taken.

A citation would be used by somebody with an interest in an estate to expedite the process of obtaining a grant where the person prima facie entitled to make the application had delayed in doing so — where, in effect, the person entitled to the grant will neither apply nor renounce so as to enable somebody else to apply.

There are three types of citation:

(a)    citation to take probate;

(b)    citation to accept or refuse a grant;

(c)    citation to propound a will.

*Citation to take probate*
A citation to take probate would be issued where an executor had been appointed under a will and had accepted office by taking some step in the administration of the estate, thereby disentitling himself from renouncing, and rendering himself bound to apply for a grant.

An executor derives title to the deceased's assets from the will. A grant of probate is merely evidence of authority to act. Therefore it is possible for an executor to take steps in administering the estate before a grant of probate is issued — this is known as 'intermeddling', and the effect is to compel an executor to act in the full administration of the estate. Therefore, if a named executor has intermeddled but fails to apply for a grant of probate within six months of the deceased's death, any person interested in the estate may serve on him a citation to take probate.

*Citation to accept or refuse a grant*
A citation to accept or refuse a grant can be issued by a person who would be entitled to a grant if the person cited were to renounce.

Therefore, it would typically be used by a person with an inferior right to a grant to force the person prima facie entitled into action, i.e. either to apply or to renounce.

This form of citation can be used at any time after the deceased's death, whether he has left a valid will or not.

For order of priority of entitlement to a grant, see Non-Contentious Probate Rules 1987, rr. 20 and 22.

*Citation to propound a will*
A citation to propound a will can be issued by a person with a contrary interest in the deceased's estate against all persons interested under the will, e.g., it may be used by a person who would be beneficially entitled to the estate if the will were declared invalid.

It is, in effect, a challenge to those interested under the will to attempt to establish its validity by applying for a grant.

*Procedure for obtaining a citation*

The person wishing to obtain a citation ('the citor') must first enter a caveat. It is then necessary to swear an affidavit verifying the material allegations upon which the application is based, and to lodge this, together with a copy of the relevant will (if any), in the probate registry.

A citation will then be issued, and this should be served personally on the person cited, unless the registrar directs otherwise.

The person cited must enter an appearance within eight days of service, otherwise the citor becomes entitled to the relief that he is seeking to achieve by the citation, i.e.

    (a)   if citation to take probate, the person cited is ordered to do so within a specified period;

    (b)   if citation to accept or refuse a grant, the citor can apply for a grant;

    (c)   if citation to propound a will, the citor can apply for a grant on the basis that the will is invalid.

If the person cited does enter an appearance he can show cause why the steps mentioned in the citation should not be taken. (Form of appearance to citation is identical to appearance to warning: see Non-Contentious Probate Rules 1987, sch. 1, form 5.)

## 7.2.6    CONTENTIOUS PROBATE PROCEEDINGS

Contentious probate proceedings are now governed by CPR, Part 49 and PD 49.

The proceedings must be begun in the Chancery Division of the High Court unless the net value of the estate does not exceed £30,000, in which case the county court has jurisdiction: County Courts Act 1984, s. 32. In practice, the majority of cases would be brought in the High Court.

The proceedings, which must be commenced by a claim form in the Chancery Division (PD 49, para. 2), will generally be brought by the named executor or other person seeking to propound a disputed will.

Every other person who claims to be entitled to administer the estate of the deceased should be made a defendant to the proceedings. Beneficiaries whose interests will be affected by the outcome are entitled to be heard and should be asked whether they wish to be joined as parties.

The normal time periods apply for service of a defence and/or counterclaim — i.e. 14 days from the service of the particulars of claim.

Default judgment proceedings do not apply. Instead, the claimant should wait until the period for service of pleadings has expired and apply to court for an order for trial (PD 49, para. 10.2). The court will then proceed to deal with the claim as if the defendant had acknowledged service — i.e. the claim will proceed to trial, despite the non-acknowledgement (para. 6).

### 7.2.6.1    Affidavits of testamentary scripts
PD 49, para. 5(1) provides as follows:

> *Unless the court otherwise directs, the claimant and every defendant who has acknowledged service of the claim form must by affidavit or witness statement:*
>     *(a)   describe any testamentary script of the deceased person, whose estate is the subject of the action, of which he has any knowledge or, if such be the case, stating that he knows of no such script, and*

*(b)   if any such script of which he has knowledge is not in his possession or under his control, giving the name and address of the person in whose possession or under whose control it is or, if such be the case, stating that he does not know the name or address of that person.*

Such affidavits or witness statements should be filed, together with any testamentary scripts in the deponent's possession, in the relevant office within 14 days after acknowledgement of service or, if no defendant acknowledges service, before an order is made for trial of the action. (The relevant office means the Chancery District Registry where the proceedings have been commenced, if the action has been started outside London, or Chancery Chambers at the RCJ, if the action has been started in London.)

### 7.2.6.2   Evidence of attesting witnesses

Another distinctive feature of probate proceedings relates to the status of an attesting witness.

A party seeking to propound the disputed will should, if possible, call one of the attesting witnesses to give evidence of due execution.

At the trial, an attesting witness has a special status, being regarded as a witness of the court, rather than a witness of the party calling him. The practical implication of this is that the attesting witness may be cross-examined by the party calling him as well as by the other parties.

Also, it appears that the rules of legal professional privilege do not apply to previous statements of the witness to solicitors concerning the execution.

### 7.2.6.3   Costs

The general principles for the award of costs apply in a probate proceedngs, i.e. costs are in the discretion of the court, and the discretion is usually exercised in accordance with the principle 'costs follow the event', i.e. the loser is ordered to pay the winner's costs (CPR, Part 44).

# INDEX